From Zero to iOS Hero

Swift Development for Kids and Teens

Etash Kalra

From Zero to iOS Hero

Swift Development for Kids and Teens

Etash Kalra

This book is for sale at http://leanpub.com/fromzerotoioshero

This version was published on 2019-01-10

Leanpub

Dedicated to Deepaksh, Sayan, and Sohil

Contents

Section A: Getting Started

In This Section

Chapter One: Introduction

It Starts With You

I want you to see yourself as a learner. You might be a middle schooler, a high schooler, the parent of an elementary student who wants to code, a college student looking to learn some new skills, or even be an avid programmer looking into a new programming language. You can be anyone. The point is, I wrote this book for you—someone who wants to learn something new. Regardless of whether you have done any programming before, I wrote this book to make it easy and exciting at the same time.

You are a student and a learner, and I am a student just like you. I know the advantages and challenges that we face in learning to program at any age. That's why I started writing with **you** in mind and wrote this book to make your journey into iOS coding as simple and engaging as possible. As a part of the *No Stoppin'* platform, this book was written for a student, by a student.

Please realize that this book is as good as what **you** make out of it. I have tried to make learning iOS Programming as easy as possible, but it will take your dedication to learn all of the concepts in this book. In the following pages, I will share some advice with you on how to make the most out of the book. I hope you have a fun time learning, and, in a while, you'll be creating some awesome apps!

About This Book and Me

As we say in programming land, *Hello World!*

Before starting our journey into learning how to code, I wanted to quickly introduce myself, and share why I wrote this book.

My name is Etash Kalra, and I'm a high school student at the Douglas County High School in Colorado. I first started to learn programming in middle school, with the Hour of Code movement started by Code.org (if you haven't already, make sure to check it out). After learning basic programming, through drag-and-drop coding, I saw the possibilities of computer science and I set out to learn more. I started learning to code using many different online resources and through some free books, I found in my library. Soon enough, after a lot of effort, I learned my first language, Java.

After learning Java and Object-Oriented Programming (which we'll talk about), I learned a few more programming languages (once you learn one, the rest are much easier to learn). I started creating iOS apps using Swift and released my first app on the App Store in 9th grade. The app was called *Spell Me!*, which helped students learn how to practice spelling and vocabulary. Later on, I submitted that app and won the Congressional App Challenge. Following that, I dived much deeper into programming, and won a scholarship to Apple's Worldwide Developer Conference (WWDC)—it was an amazing conference.

After my first several years in the world of computer science, I saw that a lot of my classmates and friends also wanted to learn to code. Professional programming books seemed daunting to them, and they had no idea where to start. Even though so many resources exist on the Internet, they are often very difficult or expensive. Seeing coding as one of the most powerful creative outlets, this obstacle for students inspired me to write this book. Through it, I hope to address a problem that still remains largely unaddressed in the world—the lack of computer science education for young learners, like yourself.

From start to end, I wrote this book for over a year, starting it as a high school junior and finishing it through my senior year. Aimed towards my fellow peers who hope to learn programming, I hope that I can teach iOS development to you in the easiest, least daunting way possible.

No matter what age or skill level you are at, by the end of this book, you will have learned everything you need so that you can start coding your creative ideas, and even publish some apps on the App Store. I hope this book exceeds your expectations, and that, by the end of it, you become closer to your goals as a learner and a creator. I also hope that your experience in learning programming inspires more students so that we can ultimately make an impact on computer science education worldwide.

What You'll Find in This Book

To best use the book, I would like to show you what is encompassed in the following pages. This book is divided into four simple sections.

Section A This section is aimed at getting you prepared for your programming journey. In addition to learning about this book, you'll also download and set up Xcode.

Section B The second section of the book is where our programming journey really begins. You'll create your very first iOS App and learn about some of the most fundamental programming structures used in Swift. Then, we will dive deeper into programming flow with these structures, followed by a chapter on application design and an end-of-section project.

Section C Section C is centered around Object-Oriented Programming (OOP), which is a set of fundamental concepts shared by Swift and many other programming languages. In this section, you'll explore many of the more intermediate and advanced concepts that Swift includes. Section C will also apply all of the OOP concepts you learn into the third iOS app (of the six in this book) that you'll create.

Section D The last section of this book will culminate all of your knowledge from the previous sections in creating even more advanced iOS applications, getting you prepared to create and possibly publish some of your ideas. Hopefully, by the end of this section, you've really gone From Zero to iOS Hero!

What do you need for this book?

First and foremost, this book requires absolutely zero experience in programming. We'll start off with some very basic programming and then build our way up to some advanced concepts and technologies. That being said, if you already know some iOS programming, feel free to skip around in the book. If you know other programming languages, I recommend starting from the beginning to become familiar with the syntax of Swift.

What you do need to know for this book is a good understanding of basic math operations, like addition, subtraction, multiplication, and division. Having a good understanding of logic (such as conditioning) will be helpful as well. In the case that you need help with anything, I strongly recommend asking a parent or teacher for help.

Also, for this book, we will be writing our code in a program called Xcode, which I'll walk you through installing in just a bit. Xcode, however, is made specifically for Mac OS, so a Mac (2009 or newer), or a Windows computer running Mac OS is required to follow along in the book. If you do not have a Mac computer, there are a few ways to get around this (by using a virtual machine), but it can be very difficult. If you do choose to do this, I would highly suggest asking a parent for help and consulting Google or YouTube.

Getting The Most Out of This Book

To get the best out of this book, both in terms of learning computer science and creating the iOS Apps, my first tip is to take the time to fully read each section and subsection carefully. I've also included text blocks (blurbs), such as the one below to give important tips, common errors, etc. Be sure to also read those as you read this book.

 Information
This is an informational text block. Some people call this a blurb.

Additionally, with each concept covered, it is imperative that you try out the code examples on your own. Whenever there is a code snippet, take the time to understand what each line does, and try it out on your own device. I highly recommend trying to use each Swift concept in a blank Swift file (called a Playground, as you'll learn) that you update as you progress throughout each chapter. Most chapters also have an end-of-section project or some practice questions to test your knowledge of the content. I highly recommend spending a good amount of time on these, so that you can effectively apply all the knowledge you learn in the chapter.

Lastly, ask for help! Some concepts in this book may need some extra clarification or guidance, so learning them might require help. Ask parents, teachers, and fellow friends if you're stuck. You can also find myriads of online forums, such as Stack and Apple's developer forums that address many common questions that might arise.

Acknowledgements

From Zero to iOS Hero would never have been possible without the support of dozens of people. I would like to thank those who have been so supportive of me in my journey of writing this book.

I'd first like to thank my mentor, Moksh Jawa, for continually providing me support and advice on this book. From proofreading every chapter and helping with the publishing process to keeping me on my feet throughout the entire process, I cannot give enough appreciation for his unwavering support.

A sincere thank you to Aimee Drury and Michael King, my library volunteer coordinators, who invigorated my dedication to service and who supported my initiative to teach free programming classes at the Parker Library.

Thank you to Dr. Aric Sanders at the National Institute of Standards and Technology for the opportunity to work with you on some amazing projects. It was an absolutely incredible experience working at NIST and seeing the power of computer science.

To my Douglas County High Principal, Mr. Anthony Kappas, thank you for supporting my endeavors as a student.

To all of my teachers in the IB program, thank you for igniting my sense of curiosity and my love of learning.

Thank you to the Congressional App Challenge team for inspiring students like myself to learn and share our enthusiasm for computer science across the United States.

To Code.org and the Hour of Code initiative, thank you for introducing me to the world of computer science.

Thanks to the Kindle Direct Publishing and LeanPub platforms for being wonderful tools for anyone like me to write and publish books.

A huge thank you to my little brother, Deepaksh, and cousins, Sayan and Sohil, for serving as the inspiration for this book. My motivation for writing this was possible only because of the enthusiasm of young learners like yourselves.

Most importantly, I'm eternally grateful for my family's support: my mom, dad, Dada ji, Dadi ji, Nana ji, Nani ji, and (again) my little brother Deepaksh in their unfaltering encouragement and strength.

Lastly, thank you to each of my friends, teachers, relatives, and everyone else who directly or indirectly helped with this book.

Without any of these amazing people, From Zero to iOS Hero would just be a dream. Thank you.

Etash Kalra
December 2018

Chapter Two: Setting Up Xcode

What is Xcode?

In this short chapter, you will setup Xcode, the IDE we will use for the rest of this book. An IDE (Integrated Development Environment) is a software application that allows programmers to edit, run, and test code. Xcode, like most IDEs, includes a source code editor to write Swift code, a debugger to test apps, a compiler to run apps, and an interface to build the layout of your apps. Xcode is an IDE released by Apple to make iOS, macOS, tvOS, and watchOS apps.

In Xcode's source code editor, we can type several different coding languages—the two used for iOS development are Objective-C and Swift. They are similar languages, as they are both based on a common language called C. However, Swift is a newer and higher performing language and known to be much easier to learn, so we will be writing all of our code in Swift.

Installing Xcode

1) Once you have started up your Mac, go to `https://developer.apple.com/download/`.

2) After navigating to the link, you will be prompted to enter your Apple ID and password. If you are under 18, you can use your parent or guardians' Apple ID for this. If neither you nor your parent has an Apple ID, create one on the same screen "Create Apple ID" and then sign in to continue downloading Xcode.

3) Press "Download" on the latest Xcode version that appears on the Downloads page (do not download a "beta" version). As of writing this book, Xcode 9.4.1 is the latest non-beta version.

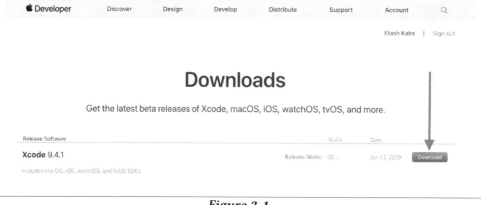

Figure 2-1

Since this book was written with Xcode 9, newer IDE releases may appear and function differently. To download older versions of Xcode 9, go to `https://developer.apple.com/download/more` and download the respective version.

4) Clicking "Download" will then launch the Mac App Store on your computer. After signing into the App Store, the Xcode App Page will show up. On that page, press "Get" or "Install" and continue the download.

Figure 2-2

 If you are downloading a non-current release of Xcode (Xcode 9), simply download the `.xip` file from the specified link in Step 3, and double-click the downloaded file to uncompress it and install Xcode. See *Figure 2-3*.

Figure 2-3

5) Follow the Xcode instructions to sign into your developer account and finish setting up the Xcode IDE.

Section B: Learning the Basics

In This Section

Chapter Three: Your Very First App

Creating a New Project

Now that we have successfully installed Xcode, let's create our first iOS app!

1) Open Xcode. You can navigate to it by opening Finder, selecting the "Applications" tab, and opening the Xcode application.

2) Once Xcode has started, create a new project. You can do this in one of two ways:

a) Xcode will open a "Welcome to Xcode" screen. Select the option "Create a new Xcode Project" (See *Figure 3-1a*)

b) If the "Welcome to Xcode" screen is not open, select the Xcode icon in the dock. Then, from the toolbar at the top of the screen, navigate to File>New>Project (See *Figure 3-1b*)

| *Figure 3-1a* | *Figure 3-1b* |

3) In the new Xcode options window, select "Single View Application" and proceed.

4) In the second set of options, enter the "Product Name" of your first app (e.g. "My very first app").

5) Under Organization Name, enter your name, and make sure the team selected is that of your account.

6) Under Organization Identifier, put "com" followed by a period, and then a word such as your name.

 Every app in the App Store has a unique bundle identifier, which is your organization identifier followed by your app name. In my case, my organization ID is "com.EtashKalra" and my bundle ID for this app is "com.EtashKalra.My-Very-First-App".

7) Make sure that the language is selected as "Swift," and the app's devices are "Universal." See *Figure 3-2*.

8) Press Next, and save the project to your computer.

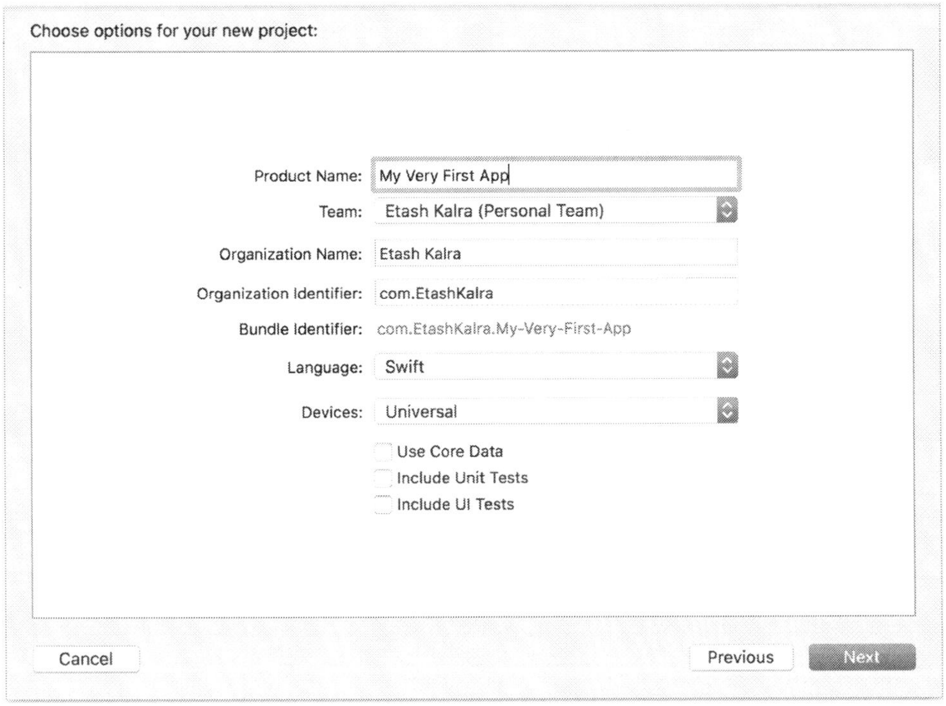

Figure 3-2

Inside Xcode

To start programming in Xcode, we must look at how to use it! The opening screen will look similar to *Figure 3-3*.

Toolbar   Editor Area

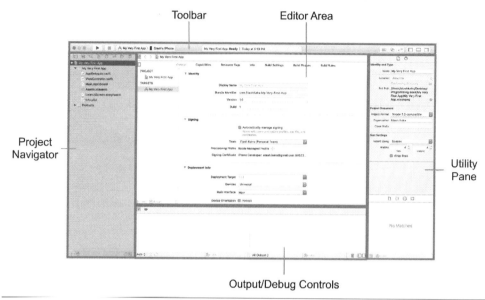

Project
Navigator

Utility
Pane

Output/Debug Controls

Figure 3-3

- **Toolbar** – The toolbar allows for controlling the views that are shown on Xcode. For instance, the buttons in *Figure 3-4* show and hide the Project Navigator, Output/Debug Controls, and the Utility Pane. The toolbar also allows for quick access to functions such as running/stopping the program, selecting a device, and the status of the project. In *Figure 3-3*, the status can be seen in the center section of the toolbar, as "Ready".

Figure 3-4

- **Project Navigator** – The project navigator pane on the left side of the screen shows all the files and resources in the current project as well as the name of the current file selected. As of now, only the default files which were created automatically are there. You can hide/show this tab using the toolbar.
- **Editor Area** – This area is the main part of the Xcode interface. It shows all of the information, code, or setup of the app (depending on which file you select in the project navigator). Try pressing the "ViewController.swift" file, and see the code that appears in this area.
- **Utility Pane** – The utility pane on the right side serves as a way to edit the information and settings of the selected file. Usually, this view is used primarily for editing information about the layout of the app on Main.storyboard (which we'll talk about shortly). Again, it can also be hidden using the buttons on the toolbar.
- **Output/Debug Controls** – These control areas allow for information about our app to be viewed, as it is running. Anything that is outputted through the app to this area is viewable in this area. The controls can also show variables and are a great tool for debugging within apps.

Creating App Layouts

Before creating an app, we have to design a layout for the app. The design includes the essential items we will see within the app (buttons, labels, images), which we will program later on. To start designing our first app, open the file Main.storyboard in the editor area. Again, to navigate to files in Xcode, make sure the project navigator is visible.

 Don't forget! The project navigator bar can be shown/hidden by using the toolbar buttons shown in *Figure 3-5*. Clicking on the left editor button in the toolbar will open the project navigator (shown in *Figure 3-5*).

Figure 3-5

 The project navigator bar can do more than select files. If you look at the top of the project navigator bar, there are many options. The first option (which looks like a folder and is selected in *Figure 3-6*) should be selected to view and select files to appear in the editor view.

Figure 3-6

The Main.storyboard file is different from other files in Xcode in that it has an interactive layout. Rather than a coding aspect, the storyboard is a visual interface where you can drag and drop items. Selecting the storyboard will also change content in the utility pane, where a library of items are available to add to your app layouts (see *Figure 3-7*).

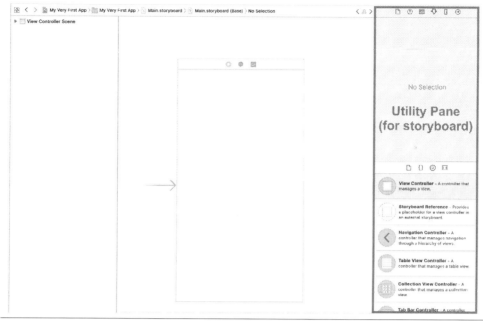

Figure 3-7

Additionally, all basic items in our app can be found in the utility pane, but access to those items (buttons, labels, etc.) lies in the object library, which is selected by pressing the third circular icon as shown in *Figure 3-8*.

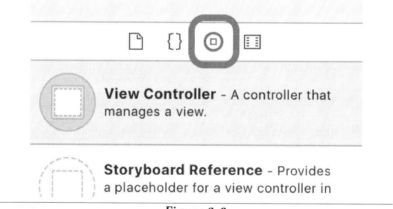

Figure 3-8

The very first app we will create is a calculator which will perform addition and subtraction on two numbers. Imagining our calculator, we need two fields to enter our two numbers, one button that says "add," another button that says "subtract," and a label to display our answer. This means, on the main screen in our storyboard, we need:

- 2 Text Fields (*Figure 3-9a*)
- 2 Buttons (*Figure 3-9b*)
- 1 Label (*Figure 3-9c*)

Text
Text Field - Displays editable text and sends an action message to a target object when Return is tapped.

Figure 3-9a

Button
Button - Intercepts touch events and sends an action message to a target object when it's tapped.

Figure 3-9b

Label
Label - A variably sized amount of static text.

Figure 3-9c

All of these items can be found in the utility pane's object library. Simply drag them from the utility pane on to the given layout in Xcode (see *Figure 3-10*).

No Selection
Object - Provides a template for objects and controllers not directly available in Interface Builder.
Label
Label - A variably sized amount of static text.
Button
Button - Intercepts touch events and sends an action message to a target object when it's tapped.

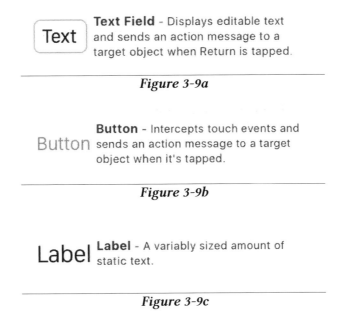

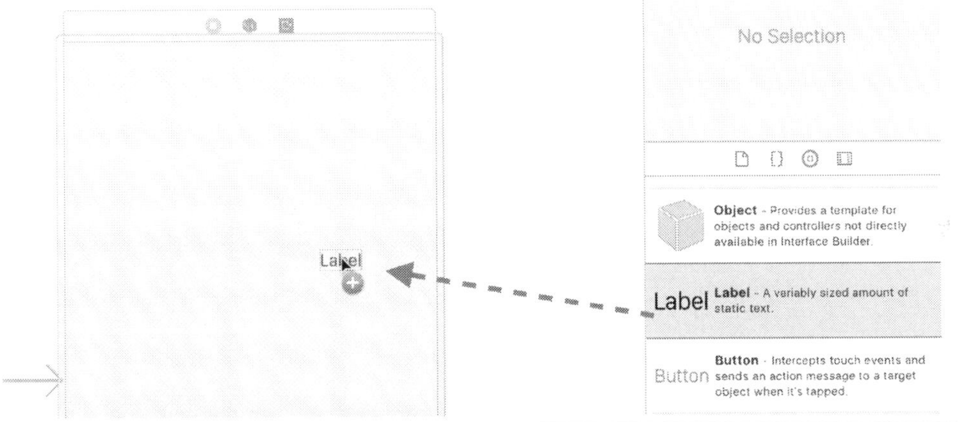

Figure 3-10

After dragging all the needed items onto the layout view, we can rename and title them using the utility pane. Simply click on the item in the storyboard, and then change the "text" for labels and the "title" for buttons (see *Figure 3-11a*).

Make sure the attributes inspector icon (carrot-like) is selected at the very top of the utility pane! If any of the other icons are selected, we won't be able to edit attributes such as text or title. See this at the top of *Figure 3-11a*.

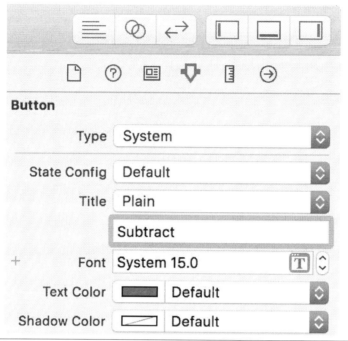

Figure 3-11a

Additionally, for the two text fields, scroll down in the utility pane and make sure the "Keyboard Type" option is selected as "Number Pad" for both, as we only want numbers in our calculator, not letters and symbols (see *Figure 3-11b*).

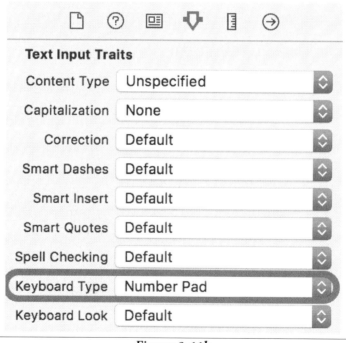

Figure 3-11b

All of the attributes for the items on the screen can be changed in the utility pane, such as color, text alignment, font, tag, etc. Try playing around with the attributes to add flavor to your app!

After dragging around and resizing the items, the layout should look similar to *Figure 3-12.*

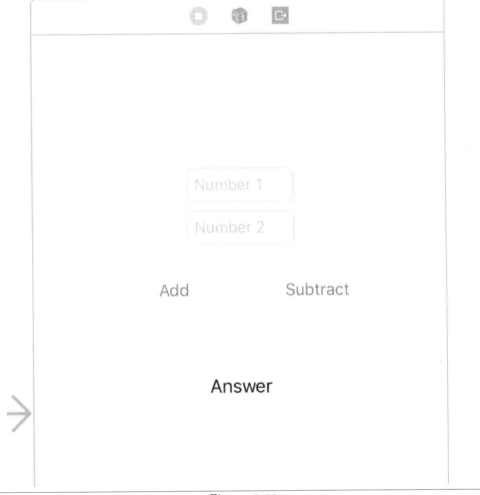

Figure 3-12

The area in which we have put all of the buttons, the text fields, and the label is called a **view**. In this case, the view is a white rectangle which encompasses the entire screen. The entire (phone) screen itself is called a **view controller** and includes components such as a status bar as well as any views that are inside it. See in *Figure 3-13* that a view controller encompasses the entire screen (including the status bar with time, battery, etc.) and can contain multiple views.

Figure 3-13

While programming in iOS, we write code for the view controller to run. The view controller can control aspects within its views. For instance, the view controller in our app can control all of the buttons, text fields, and labels in our white view.

Connecting App Layouts to Code

Each view controller has a view controller file associated with it. This file is where we write all of the Swift code to control all the items in the view controller. In essence, we are creating the view controller and its layout in the storyboard. Then, after creating and laying out the view controller, we connect a file to it and write code that controls the different items within the view controller.

The view controller that we used in our app was created default by Xcode, so it already has a `ViewController.swift` file connected to it. You can see the default file in the project navigator. However, even though the file is connected to the view controller (they correspond to each other), the code file has no way of controlling the text fields, labels, and buttons that are in `Main.storyboard`. We must connect those items to the file as well. Because these items lie *within* the view controller, we can connect them to the same `ViewController.swift` file, rather than creating new files for each button and text field. By connecting the objects to a view controller file, the code in the file has the ability to access or change those objects. Without references, the objects would just be static and non-functional.

To connect the buttons to the file, we need to first get the storyboard and the file next to each other, side-by-side in Xcode. To view two things at the same time in Xcode, we need to use the "Show assistant editor" option in the upper toolbar. See *Figure 3-14*.

Figure 3-14

This splits the editor area into two. On the left, we need to have the storyboard. On the right, we need the code file for the view controller. This can be done in the top of the editor view(s). See *Figure 3-15a* to see how to navigate files within each of these views.

 In the assistant editor mode, the navigation bar can also be used to control what is shown in the left assistant editor. If you select the `Main.storyboard`, you can select the desired view controller. Then, as shown in *Figure 3-15b*, the `Automatic` option may become visible in the right-hand assistant editor, and selecting that option will open the code file for the selected view controller.

Figure 3-15a

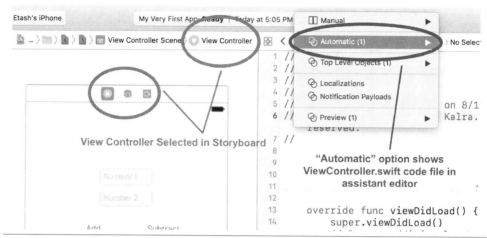

Figure 3-15b

 To save space on the screen during split view mode, remember you can hide/show the left navigation bar and the right utility bar.

Now, the buttons, text fields, and labels must be referenced in the ViewController.swift file so that the code knows which components it should change and use. In order to connect/create a reference, click on one component. For instance, click on the top text field. Then, hold the **Control** key on your keyboard, and simultaneously drag from the desired component into a place on the swift file. See *Figure 3-16* to see where to drag the component.

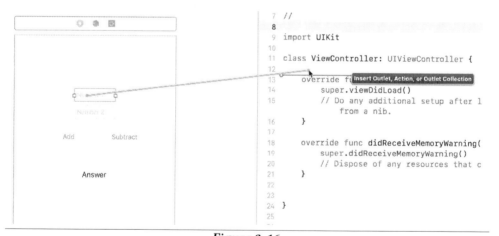

Figure 3-16

After dragging the component, an *Options* field will appear. Here you will name the text field numberOneTF. Remember that capitalization matters in programming, so O T and F should all be capitalized.

 Swift uses a naming system called camelCase, in which all words in variable or object names are put together, but the first letter of each word is uppercase (except for the first word). Here are some examples of camelCase: camelCase, variableName, myFavoriteButton.

After putting in the name, leave the rest of the options in the fields as the default options, and press "Connect." See *Figure 3-17.*

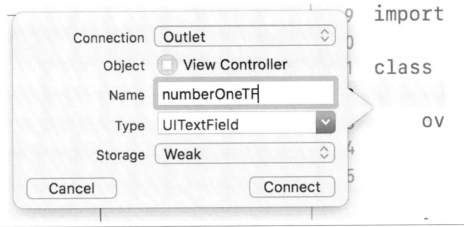

Figure 3-17

The process connects the text field to a code reference in the file, which is the following line of code:

```
1  @IBOutlet weak var numberOneTF: UITextField!
```

 Make sure the code line that is referenced is *indented* at the same level as the line that reads `override func viewDidLoad`. See *Figure 3-16* again to see the placement of the text field reference.

```
8
9  import UIKit
10
11  class ViewController: UIViewController {
12
       @IBOutlet weak var numberOneTF: UITextField!
14
15      override func viewDidLoad() {
16          super.viewDidLoad()
```

Figure 3-18

After the text field has been connected to the Swift file and referenced, as in *Figure 3-18*, proceed to reference the `numberTwoTF` (second text field) and the `answerLabel` (label). The process is the exact same as connecting the first text field (click on the item, **Control** + drag, enter a name, connect).

However, do not reference the add and subtract buttons in the code yet; buttons will be connected differently. Your code should look like *Figure 3-19.*

```
 9  import UIKit
10
11  class ViewController: UIViewController {
12
       @IBOutlet weak var numberOneTF: UITextField!
       @IBOutlet weak var numberTwoTF: UITextField!
       @IBOutlet weak var answerLabel: UILabel!
16
```

Figure 3-19

Now, a question might arise in your mind: why don't we connect the buttons to the code just like the text fields and labels? What is the difference?

If we wanted to, we could have also connected and referenced the buttons on the app layout in the same way we did the text fields and label. However, that would have referenced the button in a way that lets the computer know what the button is, and where it can find the button. **But**, simply referencing it at as an `Outlet` doesn't let Xcode know **when** the button is clicked, which is what we want it to know.

The other text fields and labels are not items that we need to get **events** from (such as when a button is clicked). They (for the most part) stay in the same state and can be accessed by referencing their name (`Outlet`). For buttons, on the other hand, we must reference an `Action` type, which is a connection that triggers a certain function when an action (i.e. clicking the button) occurs.

To do this (create an `Action` connection), click on the add button in the storyboard, and just like we did before, **Control** + drag onto a line on the code block. However, this time, change the "Connection" option to `Action` and proceed to name the connection `addClicked`. See *Figure 3-20*.

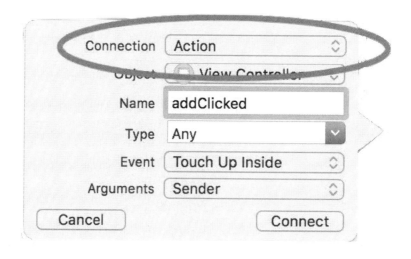

Figure 3-20

Do the same with the subtract button. Instead of outlet connections, whose lines start with `@IBOutlet`, the action connections start with `@IBAction` and continue on multiple lines with a set of opening and closing braces ({ and }).

To make your code more organized, feel free space out the code references using your cursor and the enter/return key. Blank spaces between lines don't affect your code.

```
11  class ViewController: UIViewController {
12
⊚       @IBOutlet weak var numberOneTF: UITextField!
⊚       @IBOutlet weak var numberTwoTF: UITextField!
⊚       @IBOutlet weak var answerLabel: UILabel!
16
⊚       @IBAction func addClicked(_ sender: Any) {
18       }
19
⊚       @IBAction func subtractClicked(_ sender: Any) {
21       }
22
23       override func viewDidLoad() {
24           super.viewDidLoad()
```

Figure 3-21

Starting to Code

Now that we have our app layout set up and connected to the code file, we can begin coding. Before this, let's run our app in Xcode to see where we are now.

In the toolbar, on the left-hand side, there are a group of controls *(Figure 3-22)*. These controls allow us to complete basic test functions for the app, such as select a testing device, run, and stop. Also, apps can have different schemes, such as an Apple Watch scheme, which can be selected.

Figure 3-22

In this group of options, double check the Scheme of your app is selected, and then proceed to choose a device. Notice that in the storyboard, we created the app using an iPhone 8 layout, so we will select iPhone 8 to match our layout.

 You may be wondering if we have to create a different layout for every single device. For example, if we select iPhone 8 Plus in the previous step, the layout will not look the same as on the storyboard; it will be off-center and unevenly spaced. To solve this problem, we use items called "constraints," discussed in the next section.

Press the *Run* Button. An iPhone 8 simulator will appear on the screen and run the app.

Figure 3-23

Notice that we can type into the text fields, yet pressing the buttons does nothing. Obviously, since we haven't coded anything to respond to a button click, nothing will happen! Let's get coding.

Going back to Xcode, let's first program our "add" button. The first thing we need to do is store the two numbers *temporarily* so our app can add them. To store this value, we must first create variables and assign the value inside the text field to them. Imagine variables as a box, which can hold something (or nothing). What we will do is create two boxes (variables), and then put the numbers from the text fields into the boxes (assigning a value to a variable).

To do this, type the following code inside the addClicked button function:

```
17  @IBAction func addClicked(_ sender: Any) {
18      let firstNumber = Int(numberOneTF.text)!
19      let secondNumber = Int(numberTwoTF.text)!
20  }
```

The let keyword at the beginning of each line indicates the creation of a variable. The word following the variable is the name of the variable. Remember variable names must be one word (you should use camelCase).

Then, after declaring the variable name, our variable is initialized, but it has no value (it's like an empty box). We assign a value to the variable by putting the equals (=) sign, and then a value after it. The value following the equals sign can simply be a number, a letter, a word, a statement, a Boolean (true/false), or many other types of values.

In this case, we want to get the number that is inside the text field, which is retrieved by typing the name of the text field followed by .text.

However, the "text" in the box could theoretically be anything...a number? a word? something else? To tell the compiler that the specified variable should be set as a *number*, we can put the numberOneTF.text and numberTwoTF.text expressions inside an Int (integer) cast. An Int cast specifies that the value inside of the parentheses should be converted to an integer. Simply type Int() and place the expression to be converted within the parentheses ( ), as we did above.

We now have both numbers stored in the code. All we need to do is calculate the answer. To store the answer, we create another variable and set it as the *sum* of the two numbers.

```
21      let sum = firstNumber! + secondNumber!
```

All we did was create a new variable (sum) and assign it to the sum of firstNumber and secondNumber.

 Make sure there is an exclamation point ! at the end of firstNumber and secondNumber. It is required, and will lead to an error if it is not put—we'll discuss why we need these ahead when discussing object-oriented programming.

If we go ahead and test the app now, we expect the app to add the numbers and display their sum now...except it won't.

Why not?

It won't display anything on the screen because we didn't tell it to. Yes, the computer may have added the two numbers together, but there is no code telling it to display the number.

Displaying the number is quite straightforward. Just as we used `.text` at the end of the text fields to *retrieve* the value in the text fields, we can use the same `.text` at the end of our `answerLabel` to *change* the value in the label. This time, `answerLabel.text` will be on the left hand of the equals sign, and our sum will be on the right.

```
22          answerLabel.text = String(sum)
```

Perfect! The `addClicked` function is now complete. When you type in two numbers and tap on the "Add" Button, the answer label will show the sum of the two numbers. One last thing! Just as we did earlier with the integer cast, notice we converted the sum using a String cast. A `String` represents any sequence of characters, including words, sentences, number *expressions*, etc. We'll look at variable types right after this chapter. For now, understand that labels must have Strings in them, so we had to covert the Integer to a String.

Now, let's work on the subtraction function in the app. Try to do the same things with the subtract button and compare. All we are going to change is the variable name (change `sum` to `difference`) and the math operations from add to subtract.

```
26  @IBAction func subtractClicked(_ sender: Any) {
27
28          let firstNumber = Int(numberOneTF.text)!
29          let secondNumber = Int(numberTwoTF.text)!
30
31          let difference = firstNumber! - secondNumber!
32          answerLabel.text = String(difference)
33
34  }
```

Running The App On The Simulator

The app is functionally complete now. Though there are some potential bugs that we have not addressed yet, we have written enough code for the main function of the app to be completed.

Whenever developing an app, it is important to test the app as you make progress, even before the final product is complete. Xcode has a built-in iOS simulator to test apps while coding.

Let's go ahead and test our app!

As done in *Figure 3-22* and *Figure 3-23*, we can go ahead and run the app, using the play button on the "iPhone 8" option in the left side of the toolbar.

After the simulator has booted and the app is launched, enter any two numbers into the two text fields, and observe your first iPhone app!

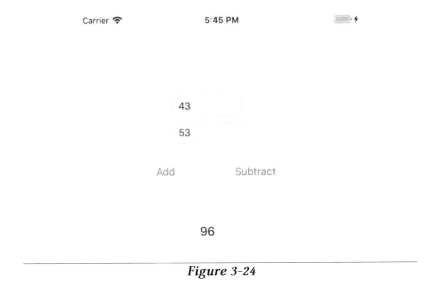

Figure 3-24

There is, however, a flaw in the app. You'll notice that if you enter nothing in either of the fields and press the "add" or "subtract" button, the app will freeze and crash. This is because the code is unable to convert the 'nothing' in the text box into a number, and cannot perform computations on 'nothing.' The issue is not addressed in the code yet, but, later in the book, we will learn how to fix this problem.

 Hint: it has to do with the ! exclamation point (called an optional) we added after `firstNumber` and `secondNumber`.

For now, give yourself a pat on the back. <u>You've created your very first iOS App!</u>

It may not seem too advanced, but you're already ten steps ahead and on your journey to creating some of the coolest apps on the App Store!

In the next chapter, we'll dive deeper into the fundamentals of programming in Swift to further your knowledge of app development.

Project Source Code

ViewController.swift

```swift
 9   import UIKit
10
11   class ViewController: UIViewController {
12
13       @IBOutlet weak var numberOneTF: UITextField!
14       @IBOutlet weak var numberTwoTF: UITextField!
15       @IBOutlet weak var answerLabel: UILabel!
16
17       @IBAction func addClicked(_ sender: Any) {
18
19           let firstNumber = Int(numberOneTF.text!)
20           let secondNumber = Int(numberTwoTF.text!)
21
22           let sum = firstNumber! + secondNumber!
23           answerLabel.text = String(sum)
24       }
25
26       @IBAction func subtractClicked(_ sender: Any) {
27
28           let firstNumber = Int(numberOneTF.text!)
29           let secondNumber = Int(numberTwoTF.text!)
30
31           let difference = firstNumber! - secondNumber!
32           answerLabel.text = String(difference)
33
34       }
35
36       override func viewDidLoad() {
37           super.viewDidLoad()
38           // Do any additional setup after loading the view, typically from a nib.
39       }
40
41       override func didReceiveMemoryWarning() {
42           super.didReceiveMemoryWarning()
43           // Dispose of any resources that can be recreated.
44       }
45   }
```

Chapter Four: Jumping into Programming Flow

Opening Playground on Xcode

Playgrounds are the second type of programming environment in Xcode, on top of the app-development/project environment we created our first app in. Playgrounds are a place where you can "play" around with code: experiment with certain code snippets, discover new functions, or just practice coding. We'll primarily be using it for the third reason: learning new programming fundamentals. In Playgrounds, you can write a short program and see the *instant* output, rather than needing to recompile the application every time some code is edited.

To open Playgrounds, launch Xcode (if it is not already open), and select the File>New>Playground option in the navigation bar at the top of your computer. If the start menu for Xcode appears, you can also select it as the first option from there. *(See Figures 4-1a/b).*

| Figure 4-1a | Figure 4-1b |

The Xcode dialogue window will now display a window for setting up the Playground. Select the iOS Playground option, and then select the "Blank" template.

Following this, name the Playground MyLearningPlayground and save it to an accessible location on your computer. A new Playground will now be launched.

Commenting

Currently, on the Playground, there are just a few lines of code. On the first line, the following code is outlined in green:

```
1   // Playground - noun: a place where people can play
```

This line of code is actually a **non-functional** piece of code, called a comment. In other words, this comment line does **not** do anything. Comments such as this one serve as "notes" for you to annotate code throughout your programs. The comment line above will still be written in the code file, but the application compiler will ignore it. It will have no impact on the functionality of the code that precedes or follows it.

Good commenting is a basic, yet essential, part of being a good programmer.

There are two types of comments: single-line and multi-line. The first type (single-line) is shown in the example above, as the comment is only on line 1.

In Swift, single-line comments (as you can tell from the name) are those which span the length of a line. You can start a single-line comment by typing two forward slashes (//) at the beginning or middle of any line. Anything that *follows* these slashes, until the beginning of the next line, will be ignored by Xcode.

The following are a good example and a bad example of a single-line comment:

Good

```
1   // This is a good single-line
2   // comment
3
4   someCode() // Another comment here
```

Bad

```
1   // This is an incorrect single-
2   line comment because each new
3   line needs a new pair of
4   slashes to be considered a comment
```

The second type of comment, a multi-line comment, is used when a comment needs to span multiple lines. Multi-line comments are the same as single-line comments but span multiple lines, so they need indicators for the **start** and the **end**.

Multi-line comments start with a forward slash followed by an asterisk (/*) and end with an asterisk followed by a forward slash (*/). It is absolutely necessary you remember to put **both** the beginning and the end characters, else the compiler will consider all of the code to be a comment. See examples of good and bad multi-line comments:

Good

```
1   /* This is a good multi-line comment, and as you can see,
2    it runs on multiple lines */
3
4   someCode() /*hello*/ smore()
5
6   /* As you saw above, multi-line comments can even be wedged to
7   start and end on the same line, without interfering with the code
8   on that line */
```

Bad

```
1    /* This is a bad multi-line comment because I never specified
2    the end using an asterisk and a forward slash.
3
4    All the code below this will be incorrectly commented and
5    ignored by the compiler
6
7    importantCode()
8    moreCode()
9    smore()
10   ....
11   ....
12   Xcode still thinks we have a comment
```

Though commenting might be seen as unnecessary because Xcode ignores comments while executing an app, it is crucial to learning how to code, even when making production-level apps. Without documenting code, which comments allow us to do, your code would be confusing to others who review your code. Code may even confuse you if comments are not used adequately. All professional programmers extensively document their code with a *thorough* use of commenting.

Also, when you want to ignore bits of code while experimenting without deleting them entirely, you can add multi-line comment tags around the code bits to have the compiler ignore them.

You'll acquire good commenting and code documentation practices throughout the book. For now, try commenting whenever you feel it's appropriate. There's no harm in commenting too much!

Variables and Storage Types

In programming, there is a lot of information that needs to be stored, inputted, or outputted. The user will input information, the application will temporarily (or permanently) store that information, manipulate it, and then output some more information. Every app works in this fundamental way. To temporarily store information and manipulate data, we use **variables**. Previously, in the first app you created (the basic calculator), we had created multiple variables: one for each number that the user put in the text field, and one variable for the answer.

The Playground that we just opened has some code written by default. Notice line 5.

```
5    var str = "Hello, Playground"
```

This line of code is a variable declaration!

To understand what variables are, think of variables as small boxes, from which you can store, retrieve, and change small bits of information. Each of these boxes, or each variable, is assigned a **data type**, which is the type of value which it stores. Here are some common data types in Swift:

Type	Swift Name	Description	Good Uses	Incorrect Uses
String	String	Any single or series of characters that are continuously enclosed within a pair of double quotes. Any character can be set to be part of a string as long as it is within the quotes. Strings commonly contain words, letters, numbers (a number within quotes is not considered a number, but rather a string). Certain characters, such as a backslash (\) can not be used within a string, except in escape characters (discussed later).	"Hello" "Yay!?" "12345" "I'm Etash."	Happy (No Quotes) "Bye "Books\ "
Character	Character	A single letter, number, or emoji, represented in double quotes by its Unicode encoding or within its raw character.	"a" "3" "\u{1F1FA}"	"ab" "hello" 2
Integer	Int	Any whole number, negative or positive, composed of adjacent digits without any decimals in between. Int has a maximum and minimum value in Swift, which is approximately +/- 2 billion.	5 10 9800 3+10 -12	"12" 99.9 90000000000
Float Double	Float Double	Floats and Doubles are used as decimal point numbers. Doubles can accommodate more decimal precision in comparison to Floats, but Floats use less space.	10.0 0.999 3.14159 -10.1 9	10.0.1 .1

Type	Swift Name	Description	Good Uses	Incorrect Uses
Boolean	Bool	Booleans hold one of two states true or false. Booleans can also contain no value, nil. Boolean expressions can be generated and evaluate to true or false. Booleans should be fully lowercase in Swift.	true false nil	TRUE False

Several other data types, including Arrays and Dictionaries, exist within Swift and are in the next chapters.

We can create a variable two different ways. If you want to create a variable whose value can be modified later in the code, write var followed by the name of the variable, an equals sign and the initial value of the variable. Occasionally, you may have to explicitly declare the type of a variable, but, usually, the compiler can automatically assign or recognize the variable type in the declaration.

Multiple types
Some values can have more than one type! For example, "a" could either be a String *or* a Character!

camelCasing
Remember that all variable names must be written in camelCase, as spaces in variable and function names are not acceptable when programming!

Let's try creating a variable in Playground. Create a variable called myName and store your name as the value of the variable.

Hint: Your name is a word, which should be stored in a String

Defining my name variable:

```
var myName = "Etash"
```

The second way we can create a variable is by creating a **constant** variable. Regular variables can have their values changed, but constants must have their value remain constant.

Constants are created similarly to regular variables, except they are defined with the let keyword instead of var.

Let's try and create a constant in Playground. Create a constant called `pi` and store the value of Pi (3.14159) as the value of the constant variable. This variable will be stored as a Float or a Double.

```
let pi = 3.14159
```

Boolean/Conditional Statements

One of the most fundamental data types in programming is the Boolean type. Booleans, as we learned earlier, are variables with a **binary** state: either `true` or `false`. Booleans allow the program to determine whether to do something (`true`) or not (`false`). All programming decisions are made using Boolean statements/conditions.

Just as the expression 2+2 represents the integer value 4, certain expressions represent Boolean values.

The most common way in which Boolean conditions are used is to compare variable values. For instance, if I wanted to store a variable representing "my age is equal to 16", it would be represented by a Boolean (`true` or `false`). Another example would be to ask whether my height is greater than or equal to the Float `5.0`. In this case, it would evaluate to the Boolean value `true`.

 Just as (2+2) evaluates to 4 (an integer), the expression (`myAge == 16`) evaluates to `true` (a Boolean).

To perform such comparisons in Swift (equal to, greater than, less than, etc.), we use comparison operators:

Comparison Operators:

(where `a` and `b` are any two variables of the same type)

- Equal to (a `==` b)
- Not equal to (a `!=` b)
- Greater than (a `>` b)
- Less than (a `<` b)
- Greater than or equal to (a `>=` b)
- Less than or equal to (a `<=` b)

 Equal to comparison operator
Notice that the "equal to" comparison operator is **TWO** adjacent equal-to signs (==). It is a common mistake to write one equal-to sign (=) when programming a Boolean expression. However, if we only put one equal to sign (a = b instead of a == b), it would <u>set</u> the value of a to be the value of b, rather than <u>check</u> if they are the same.

When using comparison operators to compare two items (item a and item b), the two items must have the **same data type**. For example, we cannot compare the String "basketball" with the float value 2.345.

String numbers vs. Integer numbers
Note: remember the value of 3 is an integer, but the value "3" is a String (because it is enclosed in double quotes). Therefore, we cannot compare something that has a value "3" and another variable or object that has the value 3. Even though comparing both of these objects in the form 3 == "3" appears to be true, it throws an error because they are different variable types.

Exercise: Writing a Boolean Expression
Let's try out an example. In your open Playground, on the bottom, if you have not already done from earlier, create a constant variable called pi and set its value to 3.14159.

```
let pi = 3.14159
```

Now, try and write a simple Boolean expression to evaluate whether pi is greater than 3 or not. On a line underneath the pi variable declaration, write a Boolean statement that compares if pi is greater than 3.

If you need guidance, check the comparison operators just before this exercise to write the expression.

The solution for the expression:

```
10   pi > 3
```

On the Playground, the expression will be evaluated in the assistant editor for you to view, and since 3.14159 is indeed greater than 3, the evaluation of this statement will be true. Such statements (which result in an outputted Boolean) are called **conditional statements**. See *Figure 4-2*.

Figure 4-2

The statement pi > 3 is the conditional statement, and true is the evaluation of that statement.

Continuing on, there are even more operators that can be used in Swift to derive conditional statements!

Logical Operators

One of these types of operators is a logical operator, which adds one or more conditional statements together to create a final statement. The three logical operators in Swift are **NOT**, **OR**, and **AND**.

Logical "NOT" Operator

This is the easiest of the three logical operators. This operator takes an evaluated conditional statement and reverses its value. It can be used by putting an exclamation point (!) in front of a conditional statement. If the conditional statement includes any other comparison operators, put parentheses around the expression before adding this operator.

Here's a table to visualize how the logical "not" operator works:

Boolean	Result
false	!false : **true**
true	!true : **false**

```
!false // results in true
!(17 >= 16) // results in NOT true, so it evaluates to false
```

No change in boolean value
Putting this logical "not" operator does not change the original boolean, unless the variable is re-assigned. Here's an example:

```
1     // absent is set to false
2     var absent = false
3
4     // present is set to the opposite of absent: it is set to true
5     var present = !absent
6
7     // absent was not changed, it is still false
8     //whereas present is "not"-false, which is true
```

Logical "AND" Operator

The logical "AND" operator evaluates true ONLY if the two booleans it is considering are both true. To evaluate two booleans with an "AND" operator, place two ampersand symbols (&&) between them:

```
1   (aBoolean) && (anotherBoolean) == someOtherBoolean
```

Here's a table to visualize how the logical "AND" operator works:

First Boolean	Second Boolean	Result
false	false	false && false : **false**
false	true	false && true : **false**
true	false	true && false : **false**
true	true	true && true : **true**

An example of a logical "AND" operator to help you:

```
1   var canHaveAccess = (age > 16) && (height < 72)
2   // canHaveAccess is only true if
3   // age is greater than 16 (conditional statement 1)
4   // AND if height is less than 72 (conditional statement 2)
```

Logical "OR" Operator

The third and final Swift logical identifier is the "OR" operator, which is similar to the "AND" operator. The "OR" expression is true if at least one of the two booleans in the expression is true. In other words, it only returns false if both boolean values are false. To evaluate two booleans with an "OR" operator, place two vertical bar symbols (||) between them:

```
1   (aBoolean) || (anotherBoolean) == someOtherBoolean
```

Here's a table to visualize how the logical "OR" operator works:

First Boolean	Second Boolean	Result
false	false	false || false : **false**
false	true	false || true : **true**
true	false	true || false : **true**
true	true	true || true : **true**

An example of a logical "OR" operator to help you:

```
1    var canHaveAccess = (age > 16) || (completedHighSchool == true)
2    // canHaveAccess is true if either
3    // age is greater than 16 (conditional statement 1)
4    // OR if completedHighSchool true (conditional statement 2)
```

Parentheses in Conditional Statements

As seen with the logical and comparison operators, often times multiple conditional statements can be nested within other conditional statements. To reduce clutter and organize conditional statements, we use parentheses in conditional statements.

(conditional == true) is the same as conditional == true when alone.

When writing conditional statements in other conditional statements (this is called **nesting** statements), the inner parentheses are evaluated first, then the outer parentheses, and finally the items outside the parentheses.

For instance, consider conditionT to be true and conditionF to be false:

In the expression: **(conditionF) && (conditionF || conditionT)**, the result will be false, as the expressions inside parentheses are evaluated first, leading to (false) && (true) which is false.

However, if we were to remove all the parentheses, **conditionF && conditionF || conditionT**, the result will be true, because Swift evaluates left to right and will evaluate the "AND" operator first by default. Thus, the expression will become false || true which is true.

Clearly, it is very important to have parentheses! The order of operation changes with parentheses. To keep it logical, always put parentheses around what you want to be evaluated **first**.

Boolean Uses

As we discussed earlier, programming is full of decision-making. Booleans are the most fundamental level for making these decisions, so they are not only theoretically important but also practically. We use booleans in almost every decision-making structure, starting with the if/else statement. Booleans can be manipulated and created in various ways through conditional statements, either through comparison or logic operators.

If-Statements

Programming is centered around manipulating and processing the inputs of a program to perform some function. One of the fundamental code structures to perform an action depending on a certain state is the if statement.

If-statements are blocks of code that perform a certain action (or run a certain block of code) only if a certain condition (conditional statement) is `true`. For example, we may only let a user play a game if he/she is above the age of 12. In this scenario, the condition would be whether that age of the user is above 12, and the action would be allowing the game to be played.

The general setup of an if-statement is as follows:

```
1    if condition {
2        // someAction
3    }
```

The `condition` must be a conditional statement. In other words, whatever is typed in place of `condition` must evaluate to `true` or `false`. To recap the past few pages, examples of conditional statements are:

- `12 > 14` (Comparison Operator)
- `myName == "Kalra"`
- `(myAge > 16) || (isSmart)`

Let's create a mini-program to check if someone is old enough to drive. After the last few statements that you typed in the Playground, create a new variable `myAge` and assign it your age.

```
10        var myAge = 16
```

Then, using the general setup of an if-statement, type an if-statement with a conditional statement to check whether age is greater than or equal to 16. If you need help, check the list of comparison operators from earlier. Leave the lines between the two curly braces (`{` and `}`) blank.

```
10        var myAge = 16
11
12        if myAge >= 16 {
13
14        }
```

After typing the word `if` and the condition (`myAge >= 16`), follow with an open brace `{`, and close the if statement with a close brace `}`. Any code that is on the lines between these two braces will only be run only <u>if the condition is `true`</u>.

All of the code between the braces should all be **indented** one `tab` inwards relative to the start of the if-statement line. After the first brace, Xcode usually inserts an automatic indent, but always double-check to make sure that there is an indent. See the following for an example of how an if-statement should and should not be indented.

Bad

```
if condition {
thisIsSomeCode()
}
```

Good

```
if condition {
    thisIsSomeCode()
}
```

After we have put in a condition in the if-statement, let's put an **action** between the opening and closing braces. In the braces (in the **action block**), put a `print` statement to inform the user they can drive.

Between the braces, type `print` followed by an open and close parentheses: ( ). Within the parentheses, enter the String: `"You are able to drive!"`.

 Remember:
this print statement should be indented one tab past the if-statement!

```
12  if myAge >=16 {
13      print("You are able to drive!")
14  }
```

Now, depending on the age we inputted for `myAge` earlier in the code, a message may or may not appear on the bottom console (see *Figure 4-3*).

```
9
    var myAge = 16
11
12  if myAge >= 16 {
        print("You are able to drive!")
14  }
15
```

⊡ ▶

You are able to drive!

Figure 4-3

Why do I have no print message? If you wrote all of the code above, and you *didn't* have any output on the Playground, think about it. Why might this be? Even if your code has no error, there shouldn't be any output if your age was less than 16...why?

If your myAge variable was set to a number <u>less than 16</u>, there is no output or result! This is because the print command will run **only** if myAge is greater than or equal to 16. If that variable is less than 16, there will be no output.

Now, let's add another if-statement to handle the condition that myAge is less than 16 (the user <u>cannot</u> drive).

 Write another if-statement below the existing one to print "You cannot drive yet" if the myAge variable is less than 16. If you need help, remember to look at the general if-statement structure and embed that into your memory!

```
16  if myAge < 16 {
17      print("You cannot drive yet.")
18  }
```

Now, there will be an output <u>regardless</u> of whether your age was less than or greater than 16. For instance, if I set myAge to 13 on line 7, I will see the "cannot drive" output, whereas if I set myAge to 16 or 17, I'll get the "you can drive" message! Check it out on the bottom of your Playground screen.

Else-Statements

Even though the second if-statement that we wrote works effectively, there is one thing about it that is redundant. Because we already checked for whether myAge was greater than or equal to 16 in the first statement, we already knew what the result of the second condition was.

If myAge >= 16 is false, then we can **guarantee** than myAge < 16 is true (and vice versa). The first condition and the second condition can never both be true. One of them is definitely true, and the other is definitely false.

Swift tackles redundancies like these with else-statements. Instead of checking the same condition in the opposite tense, we can write an else-statement. An else-statement is another statement that is added on to the end of an if-statement. Whatever is within the else { } braces is only executed if the if-statement condition is false. This combination of an if-statement followed by an else-statement is called an if-else-statement.

It works in this general setup:

```
if condition {
    doSomething()
} else {
    doSomethingElse()
}
```

Using this pattern, let's rewrite the second if-statement you wrote just before this and convert it into an else-statement. By using an if-else structure instead of two separate if-statements, the computer is doing half the computations, the code is shorter, and it's more organized!

To combine **two opposite if-statements** (we wrote earlier) into **one if-else structure**, we need to remove the `if condition` clause on the second statement, and replace it with the word `else`. Then, for formatting purposes, shift the else-block to begin on the same line that the if-block ends on.

Before

```
12  if myAge >=16 {
13      print("You are able to drive.")
14  }
15  if myAge < 16 {
16      print("You cannot drive yet.")
17  }
```

After

```
12  if myAge >=16 {
13      print("You are able to drive.")
14  } else { // myAge MUST be less than 16, because it is not greater
15      print("You cannot drive yet.")
16  }
```

Now, the Playground (which automatically refreshes) will display the same result as before, except it will do it more efficiently and with a more organized technique.

The Xcode application will now only check if `myAge >= 16`. If it is `true`, then it will print `"You are able to drive"`. Otherwise, if the expression is false, then we know that `myAge` is definitely less than 16, and it will print `"You cannot drive yet"`.

The compiler is <u>required</u> to choose **one** of the two blocks in the if-else sequence (blocks are the bits of code that are between the opening and closing braces). It chooses the if-block or the else-block depending on the conditional statement that we put in it.

Else-if-Statements

Seeing that the if-else-structure only supports two options (an `if` clause and an `else` clause), what would we do if we wanted to have *more than two* options?

Take, for example, that we also wanted to let the user know that they can have a driver's permit if they are exactly 15-years-old? This extra condition would result in three potential conditions:

(`myAge < 16`), (`myAge == 15`), and (`myAge >=16`)

Conveniently, we can support three conditions using if-else statements.

First, in our initial if-statement, we'll check if `myAge >= 16` as we had earlier. In this way, we either know if `myAge >=16` or not (`myAge < 16`). Then, after the if-statement, we'll put in another condition in an "`else if`" block to check if `myAge == 15`.

If the original `myAge > 16` condition is `false` we **definitely** know that `myAge < 16`. Now, the second block (`else if` block) should check if `myAge == 15`.

If the `myAge == 15` condition is `true`, it will output a `print` statement saying `"You can have a permit!"`.

However, if this condition is also `false`, we know that `myAge` is less than 16, and it is also **not** equal to 15. Logically, then if both conditions fail, then we know for **certain** than `myAge` is less than 15 (if both are false, our final `else` statement will output that the user cannot drive).

This `if` + `else if` + `else` combination works very similarly to the `if-else` block. See how it works:

```
12    if myAge >= 16 {
13        print("You are able to drive.")
14    } else if myAge == 15 {
15        print("You can have a permit.")
16    } else {
17        print("You cannot drive yet.")
18    }
```

Briefly, here's how the three blocks above work:

- If the `myAge >= 16` condition on line 12 is `true`, the compiler will execute line 14 and exit the structure.
- However, if `myAge >= 16` is `false`, then it will check the `myAge == 15` condition on line 16. If the `else if` condition is `true`, the compiler will execute line 18 and exit the structure.
- If `myAge >= 16` (line 12) is `false` AND `myAge == 15` (line 16) is `false`, then the compiler will execute the code in the `else` block (line 22).

Else if statements can be added an infinite number of times. That way, you can check for an unlimited number of cases. In the end, if these structures are written right, only one of the conditions should be true, so only one block will run. The code block that runs may be the initial if-statement block, it may be the first else if block, the second else if block, and so on. If **every** condition is false, Xcode resorts to running the else block.

Using the following structure for if-else if-else blocks, go ahead and try to create your own:

```
1   if condition1 {
2       doSomething()
3   } else if condition2 {
4       doAnotherThing()
5   } else if condition3 {
6       doSomethingElse()
7   } else {
8       doThis()
9   }
```

In this type of pattern, remember only one block of code will be executed.

Chapter Summary

In this chapter, we learned a lot of about programming flow and decision making (when or when not should to compiler run a piece of code). To recap all that we went over in this chapter:

- About Xcode Playgrounds
- How to write single-line and multi-line comments
- Variable types in Swift, including Strings, Characters, Integers, Booleans, etc.
- A deep look into Booleans and Conditional Statements/Expressions
- Logical and Comparison Operators in Conditional Statements
- If, Else, and Else If statements

All of these tools are the foundation for your journey in developing iOS Apps. Decision making and program flow via if-statements and the like are extremely common and necessary when developing apps. We'll start looking more at other ways of decision making and programming in the next chapter, including for-loops, while-loops, arrays, and dictionaries. Make sure to complete the following end-of-chapter exercises to practice what we just learned and play around in the Playground using the programming topics in this chapter!

End-of-Chapter Exercises

1) Which of the following is not an acceptable Swift comment?

```
(A)  // My name is Etash Kalra
     // I love to create apps!
```

```
(B)  /* My name is Etash Kalra
     I love to create apps! */
```

```
(C)  // My name is Etash Kalra
     I love to create apps! //
```

```
(D)  /*
     My name is Etash Kalra
     I love to create apps!
     */
```

2) Which of the following is an acceptable Swift boolean?

(A) `True`

(B) `false`

(C) `TRUE`

(D) `false()`

3) Integers can also be decimal numbers.

(A) True

(B) False

4) Which character interrupts the flow of a String?

(A) \ (Backslash)

(B) / (Forward slash)

(C) ~ (Tilde)

(D) # (Number sign)

5) The expression "2" could be a(n) [Select Two]:

(A) Integer

(B) Character

(C) String

(D) Float

6) The expression (2+4) could be a(n) [Select Two]:

(A) Integer

(B) String

(C) Float

(D) Character

7) The Logical 'AND' operator is written as:

(A) ||

(B) !!

(C) &&

(D) &

8) Which is not an acceptable boolean expression?

(A) `(true || false && false)`

(B) `(false || !(true && false))`

(C) `(true && (true || false && !false))`

(D) `(false && (true || false && !(false))`

9) Which of the following is a correct if, else if, else statement?

```
(A) if shoeSize = 10 {
        print("We have one pair of shoes left!")
    } else if shoeSize = 11 {
        print("We don't have any more shoes for you.")
    } else {
        print("We have shoes for you!")
    }
```

```
(B) if shoeSize == 10 {
        print("We have one pair of shoes left!")
    } else if shoeSize == 11 {
        print("We don't have any more shoes for you.")
    } else {
        print("We have shoes for you!")
    }
```

```
(C) if shoeSize == 10 {
        print("We have one pair of shoes left!")
    } else--if shoeSize == 11 {
        print("We don't have any more shoes for you.")
    } else {
        print("We have shoes for you!")
    }
```

```
(D) if shoeSize = 10 {
        print("We have one pair of shoes left!")
    } else--if shoeSize = 11 {
        print("We don't have any more shoes for you.")
    } else {
        print("We have shoes for you!")
    }
```

10) Which of the following is not a valid comparison operator?

(A) =<

(B) <=

(C) !=

(D) ==

Answers

1. C
2. B
3. B
4. A
5. B, C
6. A, C
7. C
8. D
9. B
10. A

Answer Explanations

1) **(C)** Single-line comments must begin with `//` and multi-line comments must begin with `/*` and end with `*/`.

2) **(B)** The three acceptable booleans are all lowercase expressions (`true`, `false`, `nil`)

3) **(B)** All integers must be whole numbers (positive or negative) or zero.

4) **(A)** Backslashes interrupt the flow of a String and are used for escape sequences.

5) **(B,C)** Any expression with double-quotes around it specifies a String. Since the expression is only one digit/character long, it can also be a Character. However, the expression cannot be an Integer or a Float since those types do not have double-quotes around them.

6) **(A,C)** Since the expression is not encapsulated in quotes, it is not a String nor a Character. The expression evaluates to 6, which can either be an Integer or a Float value with no decimal places.

7) **(C)** The three logical operators are `||` (OR), `&&` (AND), and `!` (NOT).

8) **(D)** Option D has three opening parentheses but only two closing parentheses. Every expression must have an equivalent number of opening and closing parentheses.

9) **(B)** Options A and D are incorrect since `shoeSize = 10` is not a boolean expression since "equal to" boolean expressions must use a double-equal-to (`==`). Options C and D are incorrect since an `else if` expression does not require dashes between `else` and `if`.

10) **(A)** Valid comparison operators include:

- `==` (equal to)
- `!=` (not equal to)
- `>` (greater than)
- `<` (less than)
- `>=` (greater than or equal)
- `<=` (less than or equal)

Chapter Five: Programming Flow With Loops and Lists

Introduction

In the previous chapter, we went over the fundamental structures for programming flow: if and else structures, which execute certain code snippets based on conditions.

There are several more ways of executing code in programming, including "loop" structures. The two Swift looping structures are `while` loops and `for` loops. These two structures are very similar in the way that they function, but have subtle differences.

Both types of loops repeat a block of code multiple times depending on a condition. They differ in how the condition is expressed. While loops are similar to if/else statements in that they take in a boolean condition and execute depending on whether or not that condition is true. For loops, on the other hand, depend on an incremental variable (usually a number) or a variable that continuously changes value.

While Loops

For this section, open a new Playground in Xcode and save it as `"LoopsPlayground"`.

To demonstrate how while loops work, let's go ahead and create one. Because while loops have the ability to repeat code, we'll create a simple loop that repeats 10 times and prints the numbers 1 through 10.

While loops have a structure similar to if loops:

```
1   while condition {
2       doSomething()
3   }
```

In the while structure, while `condition` is `true`, the `doSomething()` code will keep executing repeatedly until the condition becomes `false`. If nothing occurs to change the `condition` to `false`, this can be extremely bad for your code, as the compiler will attempt to repeat the `while` infinite times, thus freezing Xcode and your apps/programs. This is known as an infinite loop.

In our while loop, we want to print a number (with value 1), then change the number to value 2, print it again, change the value to 3...and repeat the process until we have printed the number 10.

Let's start by declaring a variable called number and setting it equal to the value 1. This will be variable which we will print repeatedly in the loop.

```
1  var number = 1
```

 Now, we'll create our while loop. Use the general while loop structure from earlier. In the place of the condition boolean, write the boolean equivalent to "number is less than or equal to 10". Within the loop, insert a print statement printing the value of number.

```
1  var number = 1
2  /*
3  while number <= 10 {
4      print(number)
5  }
6  */
```

 Caution though! This while loop will be an infinite loop (discussed below), so enclose it within a multi-line comment (/* and */) so that the compiler ignores it!

The way the while loop is currently set up, number will always be 1, because there is no code to update its value. Therefore, number will <u>always</u> be less than 10, leading to the while loop being run an infinite number of times and printing 1 every single time. To solve this problem, we'll add a line of code that adds 1 to the value of number each time the while loop executes.

Now, we'll modify the body of the while loop to increase number by 1 each run. When number becomes 11, the while condition will become false and exit, leaving us with the numbers 1 through 10 printed in the console.

To increase the value of any variable, we can use Swift incrementors, which reassign the value of any variable by adding, subtracting, multiplying, etc. a value.

If we wanted number to increase by 1 every loop run, we would reassign the variable number to be the old number value plus 1:

```
number = number + 1
```

The code segment above works perfectly. Swift makes it even easier to increment a value on a variable. Simply type the variable to be incremented, followed by += and the number to increment by:

```
number += 1
```

It works the same way and is more concise. Insert the number incrementor in the while loop, remove the multi-line comment, and watch as the compiler prints the numbers 1 through 10 (see *Figure 5-1*).

```
1   var number = 1
2
3   while number <= 10 {
4       print(number)
5       number += 1
6   }
```

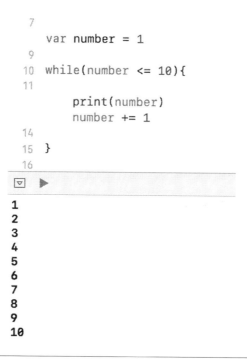

Figure 5-1

Great! We have successfully created a functioning while loop, which can loop a number from 1 to 10, printing and incrementing the number's value in each run through the loop. In the next topic, we'll discuss the second type of loop: for loops.

For Loops

While coding, we use loops *a lot*, and loop setups like the while loop we created earlier are very common. Often times, we require that code be run a certain number of times, whether it be iterating and printing 10 numbers or searching through a list.

We can use a while loop setup to run something a **predetermined** number of times, as we did in the previous example. For a while loop to do so, we need three items:

1. A counter variable. In the instance earlier, the variable number was our counter.
2. A condition dependent on the counter variable. (e.g. number <= 10)
3. An iterator/incrementor statement within the while loop to update the value of the number and avoid an infinite while loop.

For loops are an extension of while loops with these three items. For most cases of iteration, for loops are easier to use and work in the same fundamental way behind the scenes.

To demonstrate how the two loops work in the same way, we'll code a for loop to print out the numbers 1 through 10 (same example as in the while loop topic). Comment out (but don't delete) the while loop we created earlier using multi-line comments. We will start our for loop directly underneath.

Swift incorporates all three loop items above (variable declaration, condition, increment) into the first line of what we call a for or for-in loop, as so:

```
// where a is the first integer in the sequence and z is the last
// (e.g. in sequence 1 through 10, a=1, z=10)


for numberVariable in a...z {
    // doSomething
}
```

In this program, we know we want to iterate from 1 to 10. Thus, we can replace the a and the z:

```
1   for number in 1...10 {
2       // doSomething
3   }
```

And simply adding our `print` statement to the mix:

```
1    for number in 1...10 {
2        print(number)
3    }
```

There we have it! Our for loop will now print out all the numbers 1 through 10 as our while loop did! And it's so much easier this time around:

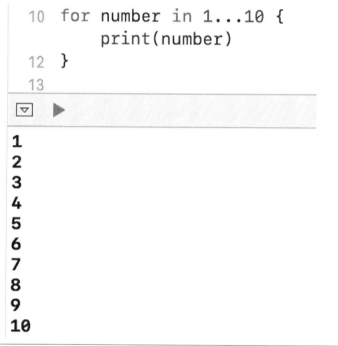

Figure 5-2

 Now that we have come up with an easier way of creating an incrementing while loop, you may wonder why while loops even exist. While loops are much broader than simply incrementing a value and repeating the loop (the task of for loops). While loops are often used in times when the stop time for the loop is unknown, whereas for loops are dependent on a known sequence. Even though we did not have an example of a while loop with an unknown stop time, we will use them in such instances the future. For now, whenever we are incrementing something a known number of times, we will use a for loop.

In addition to sequencing through ranges of numbers, for loops also can loop through lists. Lists, specifically what we call "arrays" and "dictionaries", are another fundamental part of programming. We often use for loops to read, write, or modify lists. In the next topic, we'll dive into the use of so-called "lists," specifically the types "array" and "dictionary."

Arrays and Dictionaries

As we know, lists contain multiple values within a larger entity. In Swift, we create lists by creating a variable and assigning the variable to be a collection of smaller values. For instance, we may have a list called sportsPlayed, which is stored as a variable with a collection of values "soccer", "basketball", "hockey", "football".

There are two main types of lists in Swift: Arrays and Dictionaries.

Arrays

Arrays are lists of similar items that each have a number (index) referencing where in the list they are. For example, in the sportsPlayed example earlier, if we created the list to be an array-type, "soccer" would have an index 0 (indicating it's the first item), "basketball" would have index 1 (second on the list), "hockey" would have index 2, and "football" index 3.

 Notice that an array is 0-indexed. That is, the first item in an array has an index of 0 and **not 1**. This first index as 0 is present across computer science. Make sure to remember this!

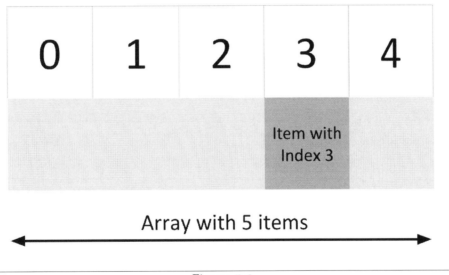

Figure 5-3

Defining Arrays

To create our first array in Swift, open a new blank Playground titled `ArraysPlayground`.

We'll define the `sportsPlayed` array we gave as an example. To define an array, start by creating a variable as we normally do:

```
1   var sportsPlayed = // something
```

Just as Strings, Integers, Booleans, and Floats are all different variable types, an Array is also a variable type, so it will be defined in the same way as other variables. We are going to be changing this array in the example, so we **do not** want it to be a `let` variable (constant variable).

Now, to define the value of the array, put all the items in the list in square brackets ([ ]), each separated by a comma:

```
["soccer", "basketball", "hockey", "football"]
```

Each of the items in our list is a String. Arrays and Dictionaries hold collections of values where each value must be of the same variable type. We could also create an array of numbers, an array of booleans, etc.

Combining our variable declaration with the array, we define our first array:

```
1   var sportsPlayed = ["soccer", "basketball", "hockey", "football"]
```

Printing, Accessing, and Adding Array Values

Now, we can print certain items in the array, or print the entire array itself.

To access a certain item on the array, put the array's name, followed by the index of the item we want to access in brackets:

```
2   sportsPlayed[3] // this corresponds to "football"
```

We can change the value of a specific item in an array just as we do with other variables:

```
3   sportsPlayed[3] = "American football"
```

We can print the item at index 3 as well:

```
4   print(sportsPlayed[3]) // prints "American football"
```

In addition to printing just one item in the list, we can also print out the entire array at once! Just put the array's name inside the print statement:

```
5   print(sportsPlayed)
```

However, this doesn't print the array in a neat way. Rather than printing each of the values in the array, the compiler prints the entire structure of the array, something that wouldn't be too helpful for us while programming.

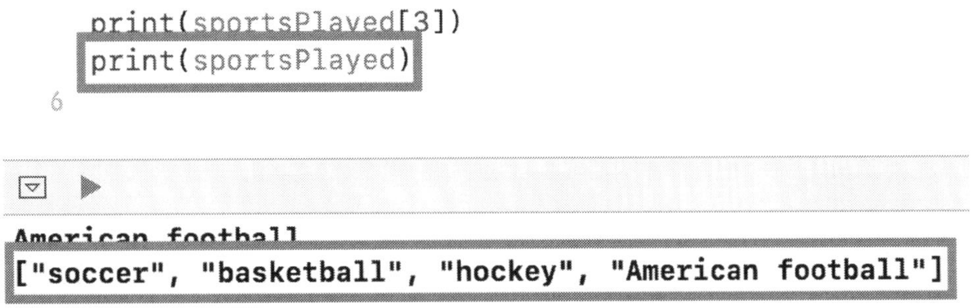

```
6   print(sportsPlayed[3])
    print(sportsPlayed)
```

```
American football
["soccer", "basketball", "hockey", "American football"]
```

Figure 5-4

To solve this problem and print all of the **raw values** in the array, replace the array print statement and print each value in the array manually:

The result is a neatly printed list of the array's values:

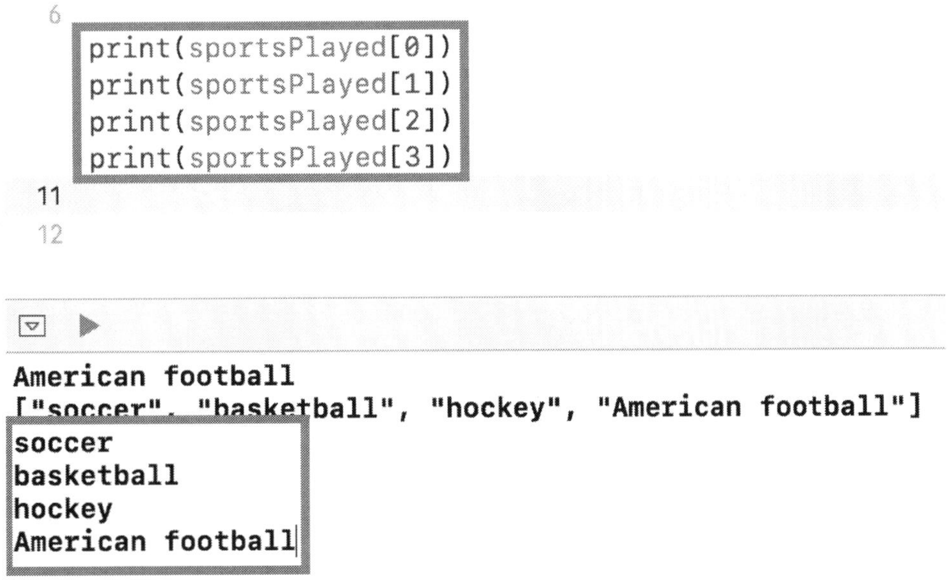

```
6   print(sportsPlayed[0])
    print(sportsPlayed[1])
    print(sportsPlayed[2])
    print(sportsPlayed[3])
11
12
```

```
American football
["soccer", "basketball", "hockey", "American football"]
soccer
basketball
hockey
American football
```

Figure 5-5

Arrays with for loops

For the last `print` example, printing every single raw value wasn't too hard. We just used four lines of code. However, how would we print out an array with hundreds of values? If we manually printed every value on a new line, the process would be a waste of time, repetitive, and inefficient.

That's where for loops come into play! We can easily print out large arrays with a for loop.

Remember that for loops often times are made to do repetitive tasks, such as printing the numbers 1 through 10. Earlier, instead of writing ten `print` statements, each with a different number, we created a for loop that sequenced through the code. We can do the same with the four array `print` lines we created above—replacing the array index (i.e. `[0]`, `[1]`, `[2]`, etc.) with the for loop iterator.

 Before we walk through how to create this for loop, try it on your own! Create a for loop that prints out every value in the `sportsPlayed` array.

First, replace the four adjacent print statements above with a basic for loop. Name the iterator variable `i` (which was `number` in the last example).

 The variable name `i` is the most commonly used and accepted variable name for for loop iterators in Swift and in other programming languages. Remember that index values start at 0!

```
7  for i in 0...3 {
8
9  }
```

All we need to do now is insert a `print` statement in the body of the for loop. The `print` statement should print the value at index `i` in the `sportsPlayed` array:

```
7  for i in 0...3 {
8      print(sportsPlayed[i])
9  }
```

 If the sequence in the for loop goes past the last index, then Swift will throw an error. For example, if we only have four items in an array, and we try to print `sportsPlayed[4]` or `sportsPlayed[5]`, Swift will throw an error.

This works! Thinking back to the scenario of having an array with hundreds of items, how could we know the number of items in the array? We knew that our `sportsPlayed` array had 4 items, so we kept our range at `0...3`.

Array Count

Swift conveniently allows us to overcome having a large array. We can find the number of items in an array with the .count attribute.

```
sportsPlayed.count // gives the value 4, as the array has four items
```

Replace the 0...3 sequence in the for loop with the sequence 0...sportsPlayed.count.

Doing so actually leads to an error. Because arrays start with the index 0, the last index in the sequence should be array.count minus 1. For example, the acceptable indices for the sportsPlayed array (with count 4) were 0 through 3.

Therefore, we need to change the for loop sequence to end at the number one less than the count of the array. There are two ways to do this:

The more obvious way–change the last value in the sequence to be the following expression:

```
(sportsPlayed.count - 1)
```

Thus, your code should look like this:

```
7   for i in 0...(sportsPlayed.count - 1) {}
```

Index Range Operators

The better way is to change the sequence from 0...sportsPlayed.count to 0..<sportsPlayed.count (use the ..< range operator rather than the ... range operator):

```
7   for i in 0..<sportsPlayed.count {}
```

The ... range operator makes the for loop go through a sequence including the first and the last number, whereas the ..< operator makes the for loop go through a sequence including the first number but not the last. Thus, it solves the problem by stopping at the value one less than sportsPlayed.count. Changing the range operator is stylistically better in Swift, but both methods work.

Even Easier For Loops with Arrays

Guess what? There's an **even easier** way to access and print array values using a for loop. Earlier, we had an iterator number (i) in the for loop, which progressed through a defined range. On top of having an iterator number, Swift supports iterator variables of any type. Instead of defining a range, we can just put the name of the array, and the iterator value will iterate through the values of the array automatically:

```
13  for sport in sportsPlayed {
14      print(sport)
15  }
```

To translate this to simple English, the for loop reads: "for each item (which we define as a sport) in the sportsPlayed array, print that sport item."

```
7  for sport in sportsPlayed {
       print(sport)
9  }
```

```
American football
["soccer", "basketball", "hockey", "American football"]
soccer
basketball
hockey
American football
```

Figure 5-6

Now, you know how to loop through arrays in two different ways. Sometimes, you'll want to have the i iterator as an integer, especially if you are accessing that number (array index) within the for loop. Other times, if the only value needed in the for loop is the actual value inside the array, you can use the for item in array format.

Adding and Removing Array Values

Arrays are extremely dynamic, or easily changeable. Often times, we'll want to add, change, or remove certain items from an array, and Swift lets us do so easily. For this part, let's clean up our Playground so we only have the original sportsPlayed array and the printing for loop:

```
⊞ < > ⬚ ArraysPlayground
    var sportsPlayed = ["soccer", "basketball", "hockey", "football"]
2
3  for sport in sportsPlayed {
       print(sport)
5  }
6
```

Figure 5-7

Adding Values

To add (append) a value to an array, we use an array function called append. Type the array's name, followed by .append(). Within the parentheses, put the value to be added the array. Try adding another sport to the sportsPlayed array:

```
3   sportsPlayed.append("tennis")
```

This addition will be reflected in all lines after the append statement. The new value will be put as the last value within the array.

To add values to the *beginning* or *middle* of an array, use the insert function. To insert a value into the array at a certain point, you need to provide the new value and the index at which you want to insert the value. For example, if we were to insert "volleyball" as the second item in the list, we can use the insert function as follows:

```
5   sportsPlayed.insert("volleyball", at: 1)
```

Inserting a value does not replace the value at index 1, but rather shifts all the items after that value up one index.

Before the insert, we had values:

```
[0] soccer
[1] basketball
[2] hockey
[3] football
[4] tennis
```

And after the insert, the indices after "volleyball" shift up one.

```
[0] soccer
[1] volleyball
[2] basketball
[3] hockey
[4] football
[5] tennis
```

Removing Values

To remove a value, we need the index of the value to be removed. Let's try and remove the "hockey" item from the array.

After adding values in the example above, "hockey" is at index 3. To double check, we can use the index(of:) function to find the index of the first appearance of "hockey" in sportsPlayed:

```
1    sportsPlayed.index(of: "hockey")
```

The Playground compiler on the right-hand side shows that the index of "hockey" in the array is indeed 3:

Figure 5-8

Thus, using the value 3, the remove function can remove the value at index 3 ("hockey") from the array:

```
9    sportsPlayed.remove(at: 3)
```

We have successfully removed the value "hockey" from the sportsPlayed array. Similarly to what happened in the insert function, all the values after "hockey" will shift down one index.

Before removing index 3, we had values:

```
[0] soccer
[1] volleyball
[2] basketball
[3] hockey
[4] football
[5] tennis
```

And after index 3 was removed:

```
[0] soccer
[1] volleyball
[2] basketball
[3] football
[4] tennis
```

To see the fully printed array, with the added values and without the removed values, move the for loop we created earlier to the bottom of the Playground, which will print the array after all changes:

```
      sportsPlayed.remove(at: 3)
10
11  for sport in sportsPlayed {
        print(sport)
13  }
```

```
soccer
volleyball
basketball
football
tennis
```

Figure 5-9

These are most of the fundamental operations associated with arrays. Arrays will come up a lot in the apps that you'll be creating on your coding journey. As we start to use them more, you'll learn much more about arrays too!

Dictionaries

The second type of list used in Swift is a dictionary. Dictionaries are similar to arrays in that they can contain many values, and each of these values is accessed through an index (in dictionaries' case, through a "key").

With arrays, we have the general set where an index (of integer type) corresponds to a specific value (of any variable type). Array indices start at 0 and increase for each value in the array.

On the other hand, instead of having integer-type indices for accessing values, dictionaries have "keys" of <u>any</u> type that are associated with the values that the dictionary stores.

For example, a phonebook can be represented by a dictionary in Swift. The name of each person in the dictionary would be the **key**, and the phone numbers would be the **values** for each of the keys.

To create a dictionary, we enclose **key-value pairs** in square brackets, similar to how we enclosed array values while defining an array. Each key-value pair is in the format `key:value`, with each pair separated by commas:

```
var myDictionary = [key1:value1, key2:value2, ....]
```

Let's try creating a phonebook dictionary. Our keys will be people's names (Strings) and the values will be their respective phone numbers—also Strings (not Integers since phone numbers contain dashes).

Create a new Playground called `DictionariesPlayground`:

```
1  var phonebook = ["Etash": "111-222-3344", "Adam": "555-666-7788"]
```

Relatively, dictionaries are extremely easy to use. To access any of the values in a dictionary, just put the name of the dictionary, followed by the specified object key in square brackets:

```
2  print(phonebook["Etash"]) //prints "111-222-3344"
```

Values can also be modified by setting the dictionary value reference equal to a new value:

```
2  phonebook["Adam"] = "987-654-3210"
```

Values in dictionaries are added in the same exact way as they are modified. Because dictionaries are unlike arrays in the fact that they do not store values in any specific order, we can just add a new value in the same way as modifying an existing one:

```
3  phonebook["Betty"] = "314-159-2654"
```

Dictionaries and For Loops

Similarly to how all array values could be accessed using the `for item in array` syntax, all dictionary key-value pairs can be accessed using for loops as well:

```
for (key, value) in dictionary {...}
```

Let's print out all of the keys (names) and values (numbers) in our dictionaries in this format:

```
Etash's number is 111-222-3344
Adam's number is 987-654-3210
Betty's number is 314-159-2654
```

First, we'll create the dictionary-for-loop, with our keys being referenced as `names` and the values being referenced as `numbers`:

```
5  for (name, number) in phonebook {
6
7  }
```

Within the for loop, we'll print a **concatenated string**. Concatenated strings are multiple strings added together to form a longer string. For example, if we were to add "Etash" + "Kalra", we would get the string "EtashKalra". We are going to create a concatenated string inside the for loop which is composed of the current key in the loop (name), the phrase "s number is " and the current key's value in the for loop (number). All of these strings can be added using the addition sign (+):

```
5   for (name, number) in phonebook {
6       print(name + "'s number is " + number)
7   }
```

This for loop now prints a new concatenated string each run through the loop. It starts off with the current key/name in the dictionary, adds the middle of the sentence (which is the same for every loop run), and then adds the value/phone number of the current key.

```
var phoneBook = ["Etash": "720-320-0075", "Adam": "938-949-9822"]
phoneBook["Betty"] = "392-000-9988"
3
4   for (name, number) in phoneBook {
        print(name + "'s number is " + number)
6   }
7
```

```
Etash's number is 720-320-0075
Adam's number is 938-949-9822
Betty's number is 392-000-9988
```

Figure 5-10

 Notice that concatenated strings don't automatically generate spaces between the strings that make them up, so we need to add spaces in the "'s number is " string to make a cohesive sentence. Without spaces, the sentence printed would be something like: Etash's number is111-222-3344

Chapter Summary

In this chapter, we learned much more about programming flow with the while and for loops, which are powerful and eliminate repetitive tasks while coding. In addition, we learned two more variable/data types: arrays and dictionaries, which acts as lists to hold multiple values within one structure. To recap all that we went over in this chapter:

Looping

- While loops
- For loops
- Differences between the two loops

Arrays and Dictionaries

- Defining arrays
- Arrays and for loops
- Range operators, array.count
- Array manipulation (adding, removing, changing, accessing values)
- Defining dictionaries
- Dictionaries vs. Arrays
- Adding and changing dictionary values
- Dictionaries and for loops

These tools (looping, arrays, dictionaries) are essential for the rest of our journey in developing iOS apps. Looping adds significantly to the programming flow within apps, and usage of loops will be very common in the apps that you'll create, both within this book and outside. In the next chapter, we are going to go back to the Xcode project editor and look at the fundamentals of designing app layouts and designs. Our second app, *Guess the Number* is also coming up in the next and final chapter of this section. Complete the following end-of-chapter exercises to embed knowledge of loops, arrays, and dictionaries into your programming skills.

End-of-Chapter Exercises

1) If an array with 10 items was created, what index would the last item in the list have?

(A) 0

(B) 9

(C) 10

(D) 111

2) Which of the following is a proper way to write a `while` loop?

```
(A) while {condition} (
        // someCode
    )
```

```
(B) while (condition) {
        // someCode
    }
```

```
(C) while (condition) [
        // some Code
    ]
```

```
(D) while (condition) = {
        // someCode
    }
```

3) What is the output of the following for loop?

```
for i in 0..<10 {
    print(i)
}
```

(A) 1 2 3 4 5 6 7 8 9 10

(B) 1 2 3 4 5 6 7 8 9

(C) 0 1 2 3 4 5 6 7 8 9 10

(D) 0 1 2 3 4 5 6 7 8 9

4) Which of the following is a correct definition of an array?

(A) `var myArray = [true, false, true, true, false]`

(B) `var myArray = {true, false, true, true, false}`

(C) `var [myArray] = [true, false, true, true, false]`

(D) `var [myArray] = (true, false, true, true, false)`

5) Which function adds another value to an array?

(A) `.append()`

(B) `.amend()`

(C) `.add()`

(D) `.annex()`

6) Given the following array,

```
let fruitArray = ["apple", "banana", "orange", "grapes"]
```

Which two for loops will print the contents of the array properly? (Pick two answers)

```
(A)  for fruit in fruitArray {
         print(fruit)
     }
```

```
(B)  for fruit in fruitArray {
         print(fruitArray)
     }
```

```
(C)  for i in 0..<fruitArray.count {
         print(i)
     }
```

```
(D)  for i in 0..<fruitArray.count {
         print(fruitArray[i])
     }
```

7) Dictionaries can be defined in which of the following manners?

(A) `let myDictionary = ["a" = true, "b" = false, "c" = false]`

(B) `let myDictionary = ("a" = true, "b" = false, "c" = false)`

(C) `let myDictionary = ["a" : true, "b" : false, "c" : false]`

(D) `let myDictionary = ("a" : true, "b" : false, "c" : false)`

8) Consider the dictionary in the previous question was successfully created. A new key "d" and value `false` are added to the dictionary. How?

(A) `myDictionary.append("d", false)`

(B) `myDictionary["d"] = false`

(C) `myDictionary.setValue("d", false)`

(D) `myDictionary("d") = false`

9) Consider the same dictionary from questions **7** and **8**. How can we print all the key-value pairs within the dictionary?

```
(A) for i in 0..<myDictionary.count {
        print(myDictionary[i])
    }
```

```
(B) for myDictionary[key: value] {
        print(key)
        print(value)
    }
```

```
(C) for (key, value) in myDictionary {
        print(key)
        print(value)
    }
```

```
(D) for key : value in myDictionary {
        print(key)
        print(value)
    }
```

Answers

1. **B**
2. **B**
3. **D**
4. **A**
5. **A**
6. **A, D**
7. **C**
8. **B**
9. **C**

Answer Explanations

1) **(B)** Array indices start at 0. Therefore, the first item would have index 0, the second item would have index 1, and the tenth (last) item would have index 9.

2) **(B)** Option A and C are incorrect since the code block must be enclosed in curly braces, not parentheses or square brackets. Option D is incorrect since there is no = symbol between the condition and the code block.

3) **(D)** The value of i will begin at 0 and progressively increase by one until 10. However, when i reaches 10, the block will not execute, since 10 is not less than 10, as specified by the ..< operator.

4) **(A)** Array names are single expressions (without square brackets), and array values are lists of values in a pair of square brackets, separated by commas.

5) **(A)** The .append() function adds the value in the parentheses to the end of the specified array.

6) **(A,D)** Option B will print the entire array four times since the for loop will run for each item in the array and print the entire array each iteration. Option C will only print the numbers 0 1 2 3, since it prints out the index of each item, and not the value itself.

7) **(C)** Dictionaries are defined as lists enclosed by square brackets (Options B and D are incorrect). Each key and value pair must be joined by a colon (Options A and B are incorrect).

8) **(B)** New values are added to a dictionary by putting the key in square brackets next to the dictionary name and setting the expression equal to the value.

9) **(C)** Key-value pairs can be printed in for loops by placing (key, value) in in front of the array name in the for loop header.

Chapter Six: Using Layouts and Programming Flow in Your Apps (App #2)

Introduction

In the previous chapter, we added some more tools for us to utilize when developing apps with Swift. Now, we have a good basis of coding fundamentals:

- Variables and Storage Types
- Commenting
- Boolean/Conditional Statements
- If statements
- Else statements
- Else if statements
- While Loops
- For Loops
- Arrays
- Dictionaries

In this chapter, we'll look more at the different elements that are used to create layouts for our apps in Xcode, and then we'll use the programming flow techniques from Chapters 4 and 5 to create our second app!

"Guess the Number" App

In this chapter, we will create a simple "guess the number" app, in which we will generate a random number and ask the user to guess the number. We will store all of the user's guesses in an array, and when the user guesses the correct answer, we will display a message. Some fundamentals we will use while developing are different types of variables (and converting variables), conditional statements, and arrays.

Getting Started

First, launch Xcode and open a new Xcode Project (not a Playground). Select the category as "iOS" and a "Single View App".

We'll call this app "Guess the Number" and select the programming language as Swift. See *Figure 6-1* for the correct setup options.

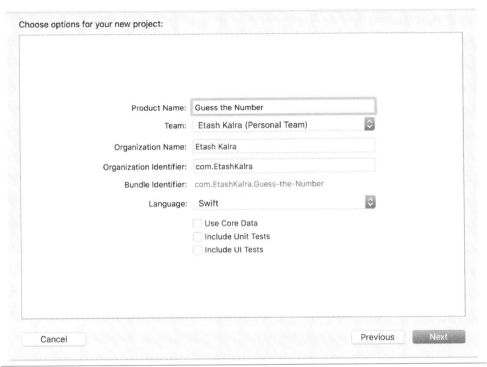

Figure 6-1

After the project view has launched, create the layout of the app first. Navigate to the Main.storyboard file in the project navigator (left) pane. In the storyboard file, there is already a default view controller in which we will create the entirety of our app. Often times, we will need multiple view controllers to create an app, but this app will only require one.

 If the project navigator (left) pane is not visible, remember you can make it open by either pressing the keys Command ⌘ and 1 or by using the buttons in the top-right-hand-side of the Xcode toolbar.

Now, we will open up the utility (right) pane. From the object library, drag a label, text field, and button onto the screen. The label will be the title of the screen, the text field will be for the user to input their guess, and the button will be to submit their guess.

In addition, drag a table view onto the view controller.

 Do not drag a `TableViewController` onto the screen, only a `TableView`!

Table views are used to display multiple items in a scrollable list-like fashion within a screen's view controller. An example of a table view is the iOS Phone app, in which Contacts appear as a scrollable list on the screen. The table view in our app will be used to display all of the user's previous guesses, so we need an Xcode object that can hold multiple values on a clean interface.

Using the resize and dragging features on the Playground, adjust the elements' sizes and positions to match the layout presented in *Figure 6-2*:

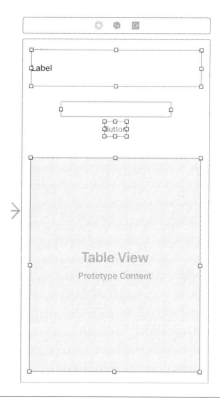

Figure 6-2

- The label should be centered and enlarged at the top of the screen.
- The text field should be directly under the label, centered and horizontally enlarged.
- The button should be directly under the text field.
- The table view should take up all the space from the bottom of the screen to the bottom of the button (with a larger gap under the button).

We have created the optimal layout for an iPhone 8 or a phone with a similar screen size. The layout size can be seen at the bottom of the storyboard file (see *Figure 6-3*).

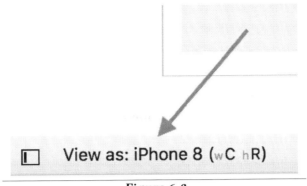

Figure 6-3

Adding Constraints

As we learned in Chapter 3, the layout for a certain device in the storyboard only stays proportional for that specific device size. In other words, the layout will only look centered and uniform if we run the app on an iPhone 8. On other devices, such as an iPhone 8 Plus, an iPhone 10, or an iPad, the app elements would be off-center.

To solve this problem, we use Xcode layout features called **constraints**. Constraints are certain rules that we place on layouts to make them more dynamic (they change size depending on the screen's dimensions). For instance, we can define a rule that certain elements must be centered on the screen regardless of screen size. In addition to dynamic constraints, we can also define the exact size of an element.

Size Constraints

In fact, let's try this size constraint out with the text field, button, and label. We can set element `height` and `width` constraints by selecting a specific element (try with the label) and then selecting the constraints button on the right-hand bottom corner of the storyboard (see *Figure 6-4*).

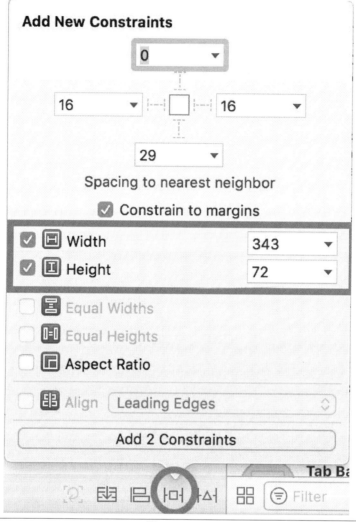

Figure 6-4

Then, check the constraint boxes next to width and height. The default values for the width and height (in terms of pixels) are the current values of the object. In *Figure 6-4* above, the label currently has a width and height of 343 and 72 pixels, so selecting "Add 2 Constraints" will add a rule that the label <u>always</u> must have those size dimensions regardless of the device it's on.

Add the same width and height constraints for the button and the text field. You can adjust the size of the elements before adding the constraints or change the width/height number in the constraint options box.

Don't add any constraints for the TableView yet though! This element will be handled a little bit differently.

If you accidentally add constraints, you can undo adding them by pressing the Command ⌘ and z keys for each unintentional constraint. Additionally, constraints can be deleted or changed by showing the layout pane and selecting the elements with constraints. The layout pane can be accessed by pressing the button in the left-hand bottom corner of the storyboard file (see *Figure 6-5*).

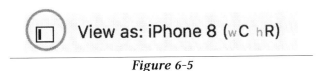

Figure 6-5

Alignment Constraints

Now, the size of the three elements will be constant on all devices. However, the positioning of these items is a larger problem. We want these items to be centered on whatever device they are on. To add a center alignment constraint, first click on the label, then press the "align" button (see *Figure 6-6*).

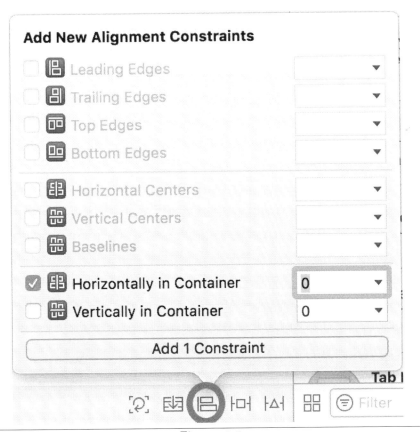

Figure 6-6

Select the horizontal alignment constraint, and leave the alignment value at 0. This aligns the label to the center of the screen. Now, align the button and the text field to the center of the screen using the same constraint feature.

Spacing Constraints

After setting size and alignment constraints for the three elements, we have made sure the following items are consistent regardless of the device:

- The size of the item
- The horizontal position of the item (placement on the "x" axis of the screen)

One item we are missing in the layout is the vertical ("y" axis) position of each of these items. We would like for the label to sit below the top of the device screen, the text field to be a certain distance below the label, and for the button to be some distance below the text field.

First, we'll add a vertical "y" constraint to the label. Pressing the same constraint button that we did for width/height, we will set a vertical constraint to bind the label to a certain distance from the top of the page (see *Figure 6-8*).

In the box at the very top of the options, enter the value 10. Adding this constraint will ensure that the top of the label will be 10 pixels below any object above it. Because there are no objects above the label, this constraint will distance the label 10 pixels from the screen margins.

 Double check the red bar underneath the upper constraint is highlighted, and the left, right, and lower constraint bars are not highlighted (*Figure 6-7*).

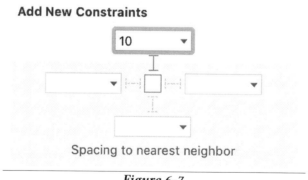

Figure 6-7

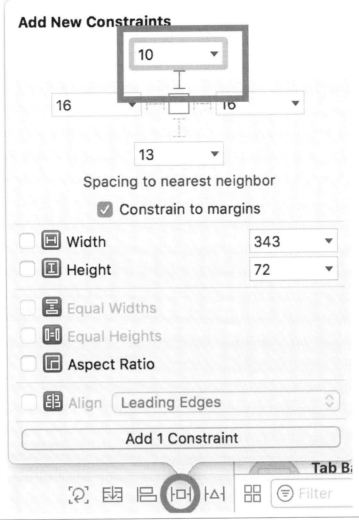

Figure 6-8

Now, add a vertical "y" constraint to the text field and the button. Each of the constraints on these other two items should be an upper constraint that spaces the item about 10-20 pixels below the item above it.

Lastly, we will add constraints to the tableView on the bottom of the View Controller. With all the other elements being constrained to the top of the screen, we want the table view to fill up any space that is left underneath the other three items. To fill up a certain space, leave the table view without any explicitly defined width or height. Rather, put upper, lower, left, and right constraints on all sides of the table view so that the table stretches or shrinks depending on the space it has around it.

Select the table view and add constraints with value 20 to all its sides:

Add New Constraints

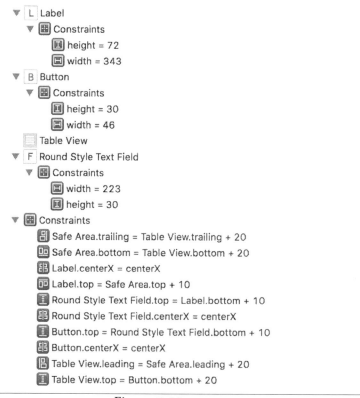

Figure 6-9

Because there were a lot of constraints involved in the four items on the screen, open the layout pane (pictured in *Figure 6-5*). Press the drop down arrows on all of the screen elements and double check with *Figure 6-10* to make sure that you have created all of the necessary constraints.

▼ L Label
   ▼ ⊞ Constraints
       ⊡ height = 72
       ⊡ width = 343
▼ B Button
   ▼ ⊞ Constraints
       ⊡ height = 30
       ⊡ width = 46
   ☐ Table View
▼ F Round Style Text Field
   ▼ ⊞ Constraints
       ⊡ width = 223
       ⊡ height = 30
▼ ⊞ Constraints
   ⊞ Safe Area.trailing = Table View.trailing + 20
   ⊞ Safe Area.bottom = Table View.bottom + 20
   ⊞ Label.centerX = centerX
   ⊞ Label.top = Safe Area.top + 10
   ⊞ Round Style Text Field.top = Label.bottom + 10
   ⊞ Round Style Text Field.centerX = centerX
   ⊞ Button.top = Round Style Text Field.bottom + 10
   ⊞ Button.centerX = centerX
   ⊞ Table View.leading = Safe Area.leading + 20
   ⊞ Table View.top = Button.bottom + 20

Figure 6-10

Perfect, if all your constraints are ready to go, we'll move on to other components necessary for setting up the layout of the app!

Finishing the Layout

After constraints, one of the largest pieces of the layout, have been completed, there are just a few more things we need to do to make the layout of our app more visually appealing. Using the Utility pane (right-hand pane) in Xcode, we can change aspects of the app elements, including the label, button, and text field.

 If the object attributes do not show up in the Utility pane, select the "carrot-like" tab in the top of the Utility page (also called the Attributes Inspector).

Modify the label by changing the text to "Guess the number!", increasing the font size, and centering the text. There are even more possibilities to design elements in the storyboard. Scrolling down on the right-hand pane, we can change the colors, border styles, tints, and other features of each element in our app. Try playing around with and customizing the title label.

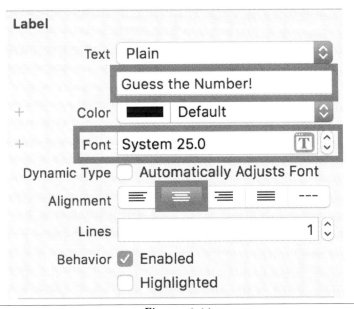

Figure 6-11

One component we must change is the text field. Under the text field attributes, in the subcategory "Text Input Traits," change the Keyboard Type to Number Pad, as we only want numbers to be entered by the user. You can also add placeholder text to the text field and change other attributes.

We can also change the font, color, or size of the button element. Make sure the text in the button is not cut off by the constraint requirements.

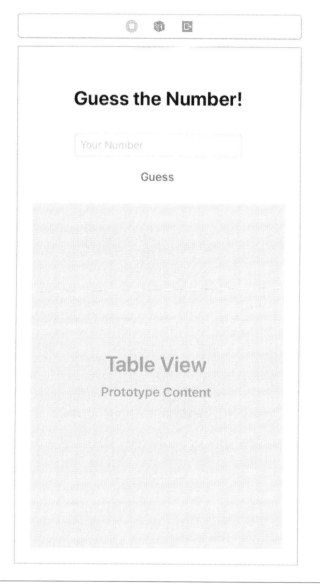

Figure 6-12

Coding the App

Connecting Items and Creating References

Now, we need to connect the items to the code so that the code that we write can access or change the objects.

Each of the objects we created will be stored as a different variable with a reference name and a value (which is a reference to the object on the storyboard file).

While you are on the storyboard screen, open the Assistant Editor view (with the Assistant Editors on the Right). This view can be opened by pressing the "Venn Diagram" button in the toolbar, and selecting the `Editors on Right` option:

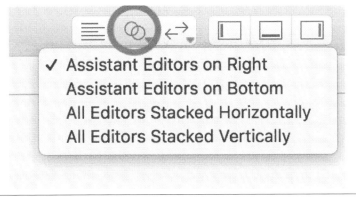

Figure 6-13

Two screens, the storyboard file (on the left) and the `ViewController.swift` file (on the right), should be open on the Xcode application. If the code file does not appear on the right side, click on the View Controller in the storyboard.

Let's connect items in the storyboard to the code file, starting with the label.

Press the label in the storyboard file to select it. Then, while pressing the **control** key, drag from the selected label to the `ViewController.swift` file.

A blue line will appear: this is where the variable will be created for the label object. Release the cursor once you have positioned the blue variable line to be beneath the `class ViewController: UIViewController` line but above the `override func viewDidLoad()` line (see *Figure 6-14*).

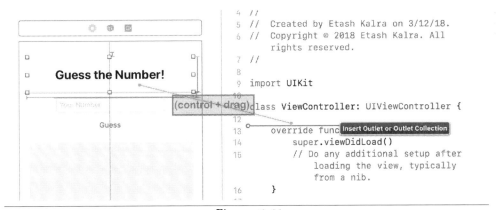

Figure 6-14

After **control**+dragging where the object should be referenced, a small options tab will appear with the attributes of the object being created. Enter `titleLabel` as the variable name and press connect.

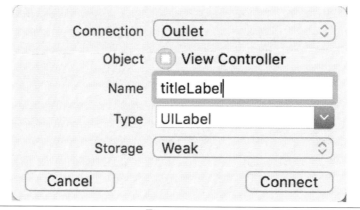

Figure 6-15

Do the same with the text field and table view, naming them `numberField` and `tableView`, respectively.

Similar to how we referenced buttons in the first app (Chapter 3), the button in this app will also be a function rather than a variable (more on functions in the next section). Let's reference the "Guess" button as a function. To do so, connect the button using **control**+drag in the same way as other objects. This time, however, instead of leaving the top option (connection type) as an `Outlet`, change it to `Action`.

This way, whenever the button is pressed, we can code certain blocks of code to be executed.

Name the button function `guessPressed`:

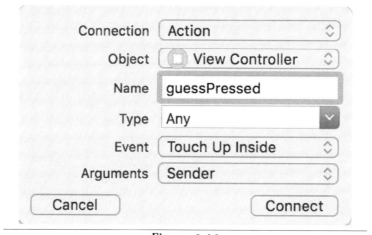

Figure 6-16

 Whenever we add a button, we need to reference it as an Action connection.

If you want to change any of the physical attributes of the button (such as font and color), create a second reference to a button in the `Outlet` form.

We can now go back to the Standard Editor view by pressing the Standard Editor button in the toolbar:

Figure 6-17

Navigate back to the ViewController.swift file in the Standard view.

As stated earlier, the connection of an object to a code file in the Outlet form will generate a variable for the object. This variable will reference the physical object in the storyboard file.

Thus, the following lines appear within the Playground:

```
13      @IBOutlet weak var titleLabel: UILabel!
14      @IBOutlet weak var numberField: UITextField!
15      @IBOutlet weak var tableView: UITableView!
```

The modifiers @IBOutlet and weak at the beginning of the line are special modifiers required for all Outlet variables. After these modifiers, there is the var keyword for variables, followed by the object/variable names (titleLabel, numberField, and tableView). After the variable name, the colon and the following word denote the **type** of variable the outlet reference should be. In addition to the generic type such as String, Int, Boolean, there are more specific types, such as UILabel, UITableView, and more.

For example, the titleLabel label we created on the storyboard is a variable of type UILabel. Rather than storing the object variables by using an equal-to sign (=) followed by an initial value, the @IBOutlet modifier automatically retrieves the value of the label.

Notice that the button is initialized differently since it is not a variable, but rather a function.

```
17      @IBAction func guessPressed(_ sender: Any) {
18      }
```

This time, the modifier in front of the object reference is @IBAction instead of @IBOutlet, indicating that a certain action must be triggered whenever the button is pressed. This action that is triggered is a **function**. The next section will dive deeper into what functions are, but, on a fundamental level, functions are blocks of code that are only run whenever they are called. They can be called from other functions, from actions (such as a button being pressed), or other blocks of code.

The basic setup of the guessPressed button function starts with the keyword func, followed by the function name, and a pair of parentheses. Inside these parentheses, we enter information called **parameters**. For now, the parameters within the parentheses won't matter. After the parentheses have been closed, there are a pair of opening and closing curly braces. Whatever code is within these two braces is the code that will be run whenever the function is triggered. Similar to the code that is between the curly braces in for and while loops, these braces and the code between them are collectively called a **code block**.

The `viewDidLoad()` Function

There are several tasks we will need to complete before the user can start using the app. The biggest task is automatically generating a random number that the user will try to guess.

Every View Controller File we create in Swift will contain a function called `viewDidLoad()` by default. This function is automatically triggered after the app starts to load, so it is used to complete any setup before the the app screen loads.

We will generate our random number in the `viewDidLoad()` function.

The default `viewDidLoad()` function:

```
20      override func viewDidLoad() {
21          super.viewDidLoad()
22          // Do any additional setup after loading the view.
23      }
```

Variable Scope

Before assigning the random number, we need to create a variable to store it. Though it is completely valid to create the number variable inside the `viewDidLoad` function, doing so will prevent the app from functioning properly.

Here's why:

Whenever a variable is created, it is assigned a **scope**. The scope of a variable controls which objects or functions have access to the variable. The scope of a variable depends on where the variable is created.

If we initialized the random number variable in `viewDidLoad()`, only items or code blocks <u>within</u> `viewDidLoad()` could access the variable. However, if the variable was created <u>outside</u> the function, then other functions, such as the `guessPressed()` function, could also access the variable, a necessity for the app to function.

Variable Scope
If a function is within the scope of a certain variable, it can access and change the value of the variable. If it is not, trying to access the variable inside of the function will lead to an error.

Thus, we will create a `numberToGuess` variable just outside the `viewDidLoad()` function. This variable will require an initial value (0), but its value updated to a random number in `viewDidLoad()`.

```
20      var numberToGuess = 0
21
22      override func viewDidLoad() {
23          super.viewDidLoad()
24          // Do any additional setup after loading the view.
25      }
```

Random Numbers

Then, in `viewDidLoad()`, reassign the value of the variable to a random number.

To generate a random number between 0 and n-1, use the following function:

`arc4random_uniform(n)` where n is an integer above 0.

Because we want our number to be a whole number (a positive integer), we will cast the output of the function to be an integer:

`Int(arc4random_uniform(n))`

Note that the random number in this function could be zero, but cannot be exactly n. Thus, if we wanted to generate a random number from 1 to 100, we could first generate an integer from 0 to 99 using `Int(arc4random_uniform(100))` and then add 1 to the expression.

Delete the comment in `viewDidLoad()` and replace it with an expression reassigning the value of `numberToGuess` to be a random number from 1 to 10:

```
22      override func viewDidLoad() {
23          super.viewDidLoad()
24          numberToGuess = Int(arc4random_uniform(10)) + 1
25      }
```

Retrieving and Evaluating the User's Guess

We will retrieve the user's guess from the `numberField` whenever the user presses the "Guess" button. When the user presses the "Guess" button, the code in the `guessPressed` function will be triggered. In this function, we can create a variable to temporarily store the user's guess and check to see if it is correct (hint: `if` statement). If the user's guess is wrong (`else` statement), we'll add the incorrect guess to a list of incorrect guesses (an array).

First, let's retrieve the user's guess. To do so, add the following line in `guessPressed` to initialize a variable with the value of `numberField.text`. The `.text` piece at the end of `numberField` is a means of accessing the text field's `text` attribute.

```
17      @IBAction func guessPressed(_ sender: Any) {
18          var userInput = numberField.text
19      }
```

One possibility we must always consider when using text fields is that the user may have left the text field blank before pushing the button. Thus, when we retrieve userInput, we must check if it is nil (empty) before proceeding.

If the userInput is empty, then it either equals the value nil or is an empty string "". Whenever we try to do something with a nil or empty value, such as convert the input to an integer, we will get an error. Therefore, we will only execute the code to check the guess if the userInput is not equal to any of the empty values.

We can check if userInput doesn't equal either of these values by using an if statement with a logical "and" operator in between. One boolean statement can check whether it is not (!=) nil and the other can check if it is not an empty string.

```
17  @IBAction func guessPressed(_ sender: Any) {
18      var userInput = numberField.text
19      if (userInput != nil) && (userInput != "") {
20          //s ome code to check the guess
21      }
22  }
```

If the user does not enter anything in the text field but presses the "Guess" button, nothing will happen. If they enter a valid value and press the button, the if block code will run.

We need to program the inside of this if statement block. As mentioned in Chapter 3, anything entered in a text field is a String value at first. Thus, the assignment of userInput = numberField.text will make the userInput variable of String type. However, we need to compare raw Integers (guess versus the actual number), not Strings, so we will need to convert (cast) the userInput String to an Integer.

Because the items entered in the numberField are Strings that are in the String form, such as "24", "49", etc., we can easily convert them to Integer types such as 24 and 49. To do so, in the if statement in the guessPressed function, add the following line of code, which creates a new variable called guessNumber and assigns it to the Integer equivalent of userInput:

```
20      if (userInput != nil) && (userInput != "") {
21          var guessNumber = Int(userInput!)
22      }
```

To convert a String to an Integer, put the String inside the parentheses of an Int() cast. Notice the exclamation point at the end of userInput. The exclamation point, known as an optional, tells the

`Int()` converter that a value **definitely** exists for `userInput`. Without the optional, the code would throw an error and crash at line 21 (more on optionals in the next section).

After creating a variable that stores the Integer value for the user's guess, add `guessNumber` to an array which stores all of the user's guesses.

The original array of guesses must be defined as an empty array outside the `guessPressed()` button function, just as the random number was originally defined outside of the `viewDidLoad()` function. Even if the array is outside of the function, we can still append values to it inside the button function.

To create a blank array, set the initial value of the variable equal to `[Int]()`, where the `Int` indicates that it is a blank array of Integer values.

```
17        var guesses = [Int]()
```

After creating the initial blank array, add the `guessNumber` to the array as our latest guess.

```
21        if (userInput != nil) && (userInput != "") {
22            var guessNumber = Int(userInput!)
23            guesses.append(guessNumber!)
24        }
```

 Note that we must add the exclamation mark (!) optional while appending the `guessNumber` as well.

After adding the `guessNumber` to the array of `guesses`, compare `guessNumber` with the actual `numberToGuess` integer.

Of course, this comparison to check if the `guessNumber` is correct will require another `if` statement. However, this new `if` statement will be <u>inside</u> of the current one. This situation, in which there are code blocks within other code blocks, is called **nesting**.

Now we will compare `guessNumber` to `numberToGuess`, checking if they are equal. If they are, we'll create an alert to tell the user that they have won. Otherwise, we'll add the incorrect guess to the array of incorrect guesses.

Create the basic `if` statement, leaving the code block empty for now.

 Equal-to operator
Remember! The "equal-to" operator is two equal-to signs (==) NOT one (=).

```
21                    if (userInput != nil) && (userInput != "") {
22                            var guessNumber = Int(userInput!)
23                            guesses.append(guessNumber!)
24                            if guessNumber == numberToGuess {
25                                    // alert the user that they have won
26                            }
27                    }
```

Add an `else` statement at the end of this nested `if` statement to handle the condition that the user's `guessNumber` was incorrect:

```
21                    if (userInput != nil) && (userInput != "") {
22                            var guessNumber = Int(userInput!)
23                            guesses.append(guessNumber!)
24                            if guessNumber == numberToGuess {
25                                    // alert the user that they have won
26                            } else {
27                                    // the user did not guess correctly
28                            }
29                    }
```

First, let's focus on the `if` block to handle the user guessing the correct number. Alert the user they have won by using and displaying an object called a `UIAlertController`. When creating this Alert Controller, set a title, which will say `"You win!"`, and message for the alert.

In the message, we will let the user know how many tries it took before they were able to guess the correct answer. The number of tries taken before the correct guess is the number of items in the `guesses` array, as each incorrect guess adds an item to the array.

To create an Alert Controller, first define a variable called `alert` in the `if` loop. This variable should be set to the value of a new `UIAlertController`, with several initial attributes, such as `title`, `message`, and `preferredStyle`. Set `title` to `"You win!"`, message to `"You took \(guesses.count) tries"`, and `preferredStyle` to `.alert`:

```
24                    if guessNumber == numberToGuess {
25                          let alert = UIAlertController(title: "You win!",
26                                  message: "You took \(guesses.count) tries!",
27                                  preferredStyle: .alert)
28                    } else {
29                          // the user did not guess correctly
30                    }
```

The `title` attribute is straightforward. In the `message` String, however, notice that there is a backslash with `guesses.count` in parentheses next to it. This backslash character is called an **escape sequence**.

Escape sequences evaluate the value between the two parentheses and place that value in the String that is outputted. That way, instead of literally printing:

`You took guesses.count tries!`

It retrieves the `guesses.count` value as if it were a piece of code and plugs that value into the String so that it prints:

`You took [n] tries!` (where `[n]` is the actual value of `guesses.count`)

Lastly, the `preferredStyle` in the `UIAlertController` is a stylistic feature, so we set it to `.alert` to make the Alert Controller be a regular alert.

Perfect. Now, we can ask the current View Controller to add the Alert Controller (named `alert`) by using the `self.present()` function. Accessing this function makes the View Controller on the screen (referring to itself as `self`) present another View on the screen.

Under the previous line, where we created and defined the `alert` variable, add another line to present this new alert controller if the user guesses correctly.

Type `self.present` and an autofill feature will appear with the option of a function called `present` with the parameters `viewControllerToPresent`, `animated`, and `completion`.

For `viewControllerToPresent`, enter `alert`, which is the variable name of the `UIAlertController`. For `animated`, enter the Boolean value `true`, and for `completion`, enter `nil`.

Thus, we should have the following `if` and `else` structure nested inside a larger `if`:

```
24      if guessNumber == numberToGuess {
25          let alert = UIAlertController(title: "You win!",
26              message: "You took \(guesses.count) tries!",
27              preferredStyle: .alert)
28
29          self.present(alert, animated: true, completion: nil)
30
31      } else {
32          // the user did not guess correctly
33      }
```

Now, when the user enters a valid value and presses guess, we will convert that guess into an integer value, which will be checked with the number to guess. If the guess is correct, an alert will appear on the screen.

We still need to address the `else` possibility though: if the user did **not** enter the correct guess. In this case, we will update the table view with each of the guesses that the user has made.

Using the Table View

To update the table view, we first must set it up. There are several functions specific to the table view, similar to `viewDidLoad()`, which create, setup, and update table views specific to some sets of options.

To access all of these functions, we need to declare that this View Controller is controlling a table view within it. To declare that our View Controller has this capability, set it as a `UITableViewDelegate` and a `UITableViewDataSource` in its class definition.

That is, at the top of our Swift file where the `class ViewController` is defined (around line 11), change the line to include the `ViewController` class as not only a `UIViewController` but also as a `UITableViewDelegate` and a `UITableViewDataSource`.

Currently, you'll see the following line set up to define the `ViewController` class:

```
11   class ViewController: UIViewController {...}
```

Add the `UITableViewDelegate` and `UITableViewDataSource` code pieces after `UIViewController`, and separate the three types by commas:

```
11   class ViewController: UIViewController, UITableViewDelegate, UITableViewDataSource {
12   ...
13   }
```

In addition, at the end of the `viewDidLoad()` function, add the following lines:

```
tableView.delegate = self
tableView.dataSource = self
```

These two lines allow the `ViewController` to control the `tableView` object and assign its data values. Section D explores this concept further.

Thus, `viewDidLoad()` will be complete with the following:

```
42   override func viewDidLoad() {
43           super.viewDidLoad()
44           numberToGuess = Int(arc4random_uniform(10)) + 1
45           tableView.delegate = self
46           tableView.dataSource = self
47   }
```

Now, we will look for an area in the class to write our table view functions. It does not matter where functions are placed, as long as they are in the `ViewController` class, because they are all called from an external source. Thus, we'll add our table view functions at the bottom of the `ViewController` class, before the closing curly brace (see *Figure 6-18*):

```
35
36              }
37          }
38      }
39
40      var numberToGuess = 0
41
42      override func viewDidLoad()
43          super.viewDidLoad()
44          numberToGuess = Int(arc4random_uniform(10)) + 1
45      }
46
47      override func didReceiveMemoryWarning() {
48          super.didReceiveMemoryWarning()
49          // Dispose of any resources that can be recreated.
50      }
51
52
53  }
```

New Table View
Functions

Figure 6-18

At this point in the code, we will write two functions. One function will tell the table view how many cells to generate (one for each item in our guesses array) and one function to tell the table view what to display in each table view cell.

Both of these functions are titled tableView() along with 50+ other functions that are named the same way. The only difference between each of these functions is the set of parameters each takes in. Thus, to access the two functions that we want, first type func tableView at the place where we want the function to be. In Xcode, a huge scrollable list of functions starting with func tableView will appear. Select the function that has the following format shown in *Figure 6-19*:

```
Tells the data source to return the number of rows in a given section of a table view.

M   tableView(_ tableView: UITableView, didSelectRowAt indexPath: IndexPath)
M   tableView(_ tableView: UITableView, didDeselectRowAt indexPath: IndexPath)
M   tableView(_ tableView: UITableView, didHighlightRowAt indexPath: IndexPath)
M   tableView(_ tableView: UITableView, didEndEditingRowAt indexPath: IndexPath?)
M   tableView(_ tableView: UITableView, didUnhighlightRowAt indexPath: IndexPath)
M   tableView(_ tableView: UITableView, canEditRowAt indexPath: IndexPath) -> Bool
M   tableView(_ tableView: UITableView, canMoveRowAt indexPath: IndexPath) -> Bool
M   tableView(_ tableView: UITableView, numberOfRowsInSection section: Int) -> Int
```

Figure 6-19

Hitting enter on this function selection, the Xcode editor now has the following function for us to use:

```
54  func tableView(_ tableView: UITableView, numberOfRowsInSection section: Int) -> Int {
55          // code
56  }
```

We will also select the tableViewFunction with the following format:

Asks the data source for a cell to insert in a particular location of the table view.

```
M tableView(_ tableView: UITableView, cellForRowAt indexPath: IndexPath) -> UITableViewCell
M tableView(_ tableView: UITableView, didSelectRowAt indexPath: IndexPath)
M tableView(_ tableView: UITableView, didDeselectRowAt indexPath: IndexPath)
M tableView(_ tableView: UITableView, didHighlightRowAt indexPath: IndexPath)
M tableView(_ tableView: UITableView, didEndEditingRowAt indexPath: IndexPath?)
M tableView(_ tableView: UITableView, didUnhighlightRowAt indexPath: IndexPath)
M tableView(_ tableView: UITableView, canEditRowAt indexPath: IndexPath) -> Bool
M tableView(_ tableView: UITableView, canMoveRowAt indexPath: IndexPath) -> Bool
```

Figure 6-20

Because we want to create one row for each item in the guesses array, in the numberOfRowsInSection function, return the number of rows that the table view should create:

```
55  func tableView(_ tableView: UITableView, numberOfRowsInSection section: Int) -> Int {
56      return guesses.count
57  }
```

In the second tableView function, cellForRowAt, the process will be slightly more complicated, but still relatively straightforward.

This function is run [n] times, where [n] is the numberOfRows we set in the previous section. For each run, it updates the cell index. So if we have 3 rows of cells, it will run with an index 0 for the first cell, index 1 for the second, and index 2 for the third. This function is similar to how for loops iterate through numbers, except it iterates through each cell index in the table view and retrieves how the cell should look and behave.

First, we need to create the entire table view cell. We did not create a template for the table view cells on the Main storyboard, so we'll use the default UITableViewCell. The cell will be created as a default cell, and then we will assign it to a variable called cell. To initialize the cell for each index, create the following variable in the function:

```
60  func tableView(_ tableView: UITableView, cellForRowAt indexPath: IndexPath) -> UITab\
61  leViewCell {
62      var cell = UITableViewCell()
63  }
```

All default UITableViewCells have a UILabel within them, which we can access. After initializing cell in the previous step, access the cell's label and set its text equal to the corresponding value in guesses.

As stated earlier, this function is run once for each table view cell index. We will access the index value for the cell and the cell's label to display the guess number for that index.

To access the row, use the expression indexPath.row. Then, plug this expression into the index for guesses as so:

(We will also need to cast the Integer type to a String, as text in labels must be a String)

```
62          var cell = UITableViewCell()
63          cell.textLabel?.text = String(guesses[indexPath.row])
```

Finally, to complete the function and submit the cell to be used in the table view, return `cell`:

```
60  func tableView(_ tableView: UITableView, cellForRowAt indexPath: IndexPath) -> UITab\
61  leViewCell {
62          var cell = UITableViewCell()
63          cell.textLabel?.text = String(guesses[indexPath.row])
64          return cell
65  }
```

Excellent. We have successfully set up the table view so that its cells will each display a guess that the user made. Though some of the concepts with functions may still seem abstract, we will discuss them more in-depth in the following sections.

For now, all we must do now is update `tableView` whenever a new guess is added to the `guesses` array. In the `else` statement in the `guessPressed()` function, write `tableView.reloadData()`. This will update the tableView with all of the incorrect guesses whenever the user guesses incorrectly.

```
     @IBAction func guessPressed(_ sender: Any) {
19          var userInput = numberField.text
20
21          if (userInput != nil) && (userInput != "") {
22              var guessNumber = Int(userInput!)
23              guesses.append(guessNumber!)
24              if guessNumber == numberToGuess {
25
26                  let alert = UIAlertController(title: "You win!",
27                      message: "You took \(guesses.count) tries!",
28                      preferredStyle: .alert)
29
30                  self.present(alert, animated: true, completion: nil)
31
32              } else {
33
34                  tableView.reloadData()
35
36              }
37          }
38      }
```

Figure 6-21

If there are warning signs on lines 19 and 22, as are in *Figure 6-21*, press the recommendation to change the `var` keyword to `let`, as the variables defined on those lines were never changed, so they can be defined either as a constant or a regular variable. Warnings do not affect the code, though, so it is not necessary to abide by warnings in every case.

Now, launch the app in the toolbar (using the play button). The Xcode simulator launches. The layout is centered and aligned, as per our constraints. If we click on the text field, a number pad will also appear. If the number pad does not appear, try pressing the **Command ⌘** and **K** keys.

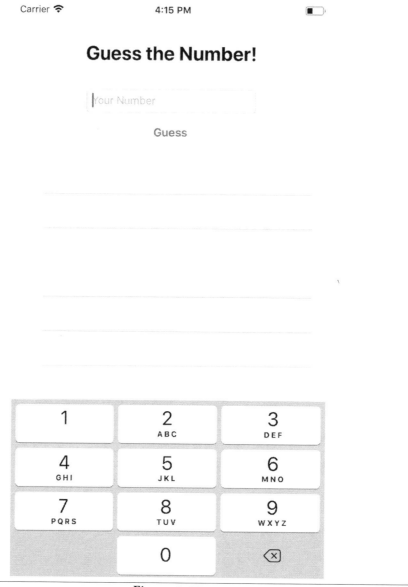

Figure 6-22

After we type a guess, if the number is not the correct guess between 1 and 10, that guess will appear on the scrollable table view. If it is correct, we'll get an alert on the screen saying that we have won in a certain number of tries.

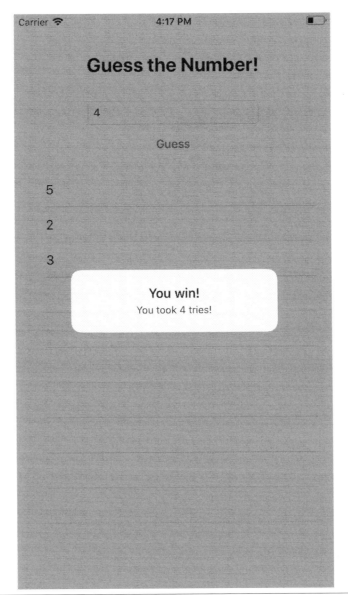

Figure 6-23

Congratulations! You've completed your second app.

As an extra challenge, try and see if you can add a text field in the app for the user to control the range of numbers in which the correct number could fall (i.e. right now the numbers being guessed are between 1-10).

If you're stuck, look at the following solution:

```
42    @IBOutlet weak var maxNumberField: UITextField!
43
44    override func viewDidLoad() {
45      super.viewDidLoad()
46
47      numberToGuess = Int(arc4random_uniform(10)) + 1
48
49      let maximumNumberText = maxNumberField.text
50
51      if (maximumNumberText != nil) && (maximimNumberText != "") {
52        let maximumNumber = Int(maximumNumberText!)
53        numberToGuess = Int(arc4random_uniform(maximumNumber!))) + 1
54      }
55
56      tableView.delegate = self
57      tableView.dataSource = self
58    }
```

Chapter Summary

In this chapter, we applied knowledge from this entire section into one app. We learned to create Xcode layouts proficiently, learned about the fundamental pieces of programming flow, and combined the two to build an application.

Because this is the end of Section B, let's recap all that we went over in this section:

- Using the Xcode interface
- Creating Simple Xcode App Layouts
- Learning how to use Xcode Playgrounds
- Commenting
- Variable Types
- Conditional Statements
- If/Else Statements
- For and While Loops
- Arrays and Dictionaries
- Creating Constraints in App Layouts
- Basic Casting/Converting Types
- Random Numbers
- Use of a Function
- `UITableView`

You are well on your way towards developing more advanced iOS apps! The next section dives into Object-Oriented Programming (OOP), which includes more integral structures in programming, including classes, functions, objects, and your third app at the end of the section.

Get ready to learn some more on our great journey of making iOS apps!

Project Source Code

ViewController.swift

```
 9   import UIKit
10
11   class ViewController: UIViewController, UITableViewDelegate, UITableViewDataSource {
12
13       @IBOutlet weak var titleLabel: UILabel!
14       @IBOutlet weak var numberField: UITextField!
15       @IBOutlet weak var tableView: UITableView!
16
17       var guesses = [Int]()
18       @IBAction func guessPressed(_ sender: Any) {
19           var userInput = numberField.text
20
21           if (userInput != nil) && (userInput != "") {
22               var guessNumber = Int(userInput!)
23               guesses.append(guessNumber!)
24               if guessNumber == numberToGuess {
25                   let alert = UIAlertController(title: "You win!",
26                       message: "You took \(guesses.count) tries!",
27                       preferredStyle: .alert)
28
29                   self.present(alert, animated: true, completion: nil)
30               } else {
31                   tableView.reloadData()
32               }
33           }
34       }
35
36       var numberToGuess = 0
37
38       @IBOutlet weak var maxNumberField: UITextField!
39
40       override func viewDidLoad() {
41           super.viewDidLoad()
42
43           numberToGuess = Int(arc4random_uniform(10)) + 1
44
45           let maximumNumberText = maxNumberField.text
46
```

```
47        if (maximumNumberText != nil) && (maximumNumberText != "") {
48            let maximumNumber = Int(maximumNumberText!)
49            numberToGuess = Int(arc4random_uniform(UInt32(maximumNumber!))) + 1
50        }
51
52        tableView.delegate = self
53        tableView.dataSource = self
54    }
55
56    override func didReceiveMemoryWarning() {
57        super.didReceiveMemoryWarning()
58        // Dispose of any resources that can be recreated.
59    }
60
61    func tableView(_ tableView: UITableView, numberOfRowsInSection section: Int) -> \
62  Int {
63        return guesses.count
64    }
65
66    func tableView(_ tableView: UITableView, cellForRowAt indexPath: IndexPath) -> U\
67  ITableViewCell {
68        var cell = UITableViewCell()
69        cell.textLabel?.text = String(guesses[indexPath.row])
70        return cell
71    }
72 }
```

Section C: Object-Oriented Programming

In This Section

Chapter Seven: Introduction to OOP

What is OOP?

This chapter aims to familiarize you with the higher-level concepts of Object-Oriented Programming (OOP). Learning and understanding OOP is necessary for programming in many programming languages, including Swift. Some of the most widely used (that are also object-oriented) programming languages today include:

- Swift (of course)
- Java
- Python
- Ruby
- Objective-C (predecessor to Swift)
- Visual Basic
- C#
- C++
- Dozens more

In this short (but sweet) chapter, we'll take a broad overview of OOP elements such as functions, variables, objects, classes, and attributes. You've already been exposed to almost all of these, but this section will broaden your knowledge of each element. Understanding OOP is also very transferrable to other languages; you're not only learning Swift in this section, but rather programming in a general sense.

After you have gained a foundational understanding of general OOP in this chapter, the following chapters will dive deeper into the specifics of each of the OOP elements, such as Functions (Chapter 8), Classes (Chapter 9), Instances and Scope (Chapter 10). In Chapter 11, you'll apply the learnings from this section in another end-of-section project.

Advantages of Object-Oriented Programming

First, let's understand what Object-Oriented Programming is and its purpose. Traditionally, programming was conducted in a straightforward step-by-step process, in which all inputs were defined in the beginning, the data would be processed, and the program would output a final result (procedural programming).

Though this process of programming may seem simple and more logical, there are several deficiencies in this linear approach. The biggest shortcoming is that the programs cannot be dynamic enough and that the process is not event-driven. For instance, in Object-Oriented Programming, whenever we need to change a certain item in a program (called an object) or change the way that a task is run (called a function), we can change the definition of the object or function, rather than changing that item or task everywhere it is used. For instance, if we have a car item (object) that we reference throughout our app and we want to change the color of the car from blue to red, we can simply change it where we define the structure of the car, rather than every place where we use the car for a certain action.

In this sense, we have compartmentalized the car's features into an "object," which is then referenced throughout the program. OOP allows us to compartmentalize specific items (objects) and tasks (functions). Everything in OOP is represented by some sort of object. Every object has a definition, or a "blueprint," which is called a class. Each class can be composed of functions, attributes, and subclasses. This way, everything is contained within a hierarchy and categorized in an organized fashion.

Whenever objects are created from "blueprint" classes, we do not need to know the implementation of how the object necessarily works. We can simply access the features of the object by providing input and receiving an output. This allows us to reuse the "compartmentalized" functions often and with ease. In older methods of programming, programmers needed to know the details for a piece of code before reusing it somewhere else, as all the code had to fit together functionally step-by-step.

Object-Oriented Programming also allows for regulation and protection of certain elements within apps. Because of the reduced need to know the implementation of a function, certain pieces of code can encapsulate themselves in a manner in which their implementations cannot be tampered with. This not only regulates and protects secure pieces of code, but also ties into the reusability and simplicity of code in OOP.

Finally, Object-Oriented Programming is much less complex than other types of programming, a difference that is especially apparent as projects become larger. It is true that on a smaller level, such as in our *Guess the Number* game, OOP requires some extra work on our part as a programmer. Once applications become much more complex, however, OOP comes to our advantage by making functions more organized and easier to utilize.

Objects, Classes, Attributes, and Functions

To facilitate the high-level concepts in this chapter, we'll use an analogy of a car.

Classes versus Objects

Imagine the concept of a car. We'll use a "blueprint" of a car to reference what **classes** are in Swift. Within Swift classes, we create the basic design of certain items in Swift, just as we would in a blueprint. However, just as a blueprint is not a physical car, a class is not a physical object; it only defines how an object will look and behave. **Objects** are the concrete form of a class. In the analogy of cars, a class would be a template or a structured plan for the car, whereas the object would be the finished, functional car after being manufactured.

Thus, within Swift and other programming languages, we say that objects are <u>instances</u> of certain classes. Without a class, we couldn't create objects, since every object requires some sort of "blueprint" that defines how it will act. Multiple objects can be created from the same class, just as multiple cars can be created from the same blueprint. Any change in the class will change the innate structure of the objects that are instances of that class.

Attributes

A car generally has four wheels, an engine, two or four doors, a color, a shape, a size, a brand, and a model number. All the physical items we just listed are **attributes**, or specific characteristics of the car. And, just as any car has specific attributes, each class has certain attributes. Each attribute in a class is stored as a variable. For instance, we may have an attribute for color stored as a String variable called `color` or an attirbute for a car's brakes stored as a boolean variable called `hasBrakes` (I'd hope this variable's value is `true`).

Some examples of attributes we have encountered are the attributes of the label class, such as `text` or `color`. The Alert Controller in the last chapter also had a `style` attribute in addition to its `title` and `message` attributes that we set.

Functions

On top of cars (classes) having attributes, classes also have **functions**. For instance, cars can turn on, turn off, speed up, slow down, turn left, turn right, etc. All of these <u>actions</u> are class functions. Functions are sets of code in a class that can be accessed and run in blocks at a time. In addition to executing a code block, functions can also receive data, output data, or both.

Input Parameters

Input parameters are specific values that are passed in (or inputted) to a function when it is run. The function typically uses the parameters to execute its code.

For instance, imagine a `speedUp()` function in the car analogy. When running the function, we need to know *how much* to increase the `speed` by. We could just set it to increase by some default value, but what if we wanted to increase by a different value every time the function was run? To solve this problem, we could add an input parameter called `amount` to the function and have the function increase the value of `speed` by `amount`. Then, each time the function is run, we could set `amount` to be however much we wanted the speed to increase by.

 Parameters are optional, however, so some functions may not have them.

Output Return

Imagine that our car object has to give information back to the user, such as the number of miles it can continue to drive. In this case, we must first calculate that value and then output it to the user. This output is called a **function return**.

When outputting a value in a function (which is optional like parameters), we define a single **return type** in the function header. Then, we can use the `return` keyword at the end of the function (there are some exceptions that we will cover later in the section) to output a specific value of a function. Functions usually return at the end of the function after all of the calculations have been made. The return type is specified in the function definition so that it knows it <u>must</u> return that specific type.

Initializer Functions

There is a type of function called an initializer, which is a function that is run whenever a new class is initialized. For example, if we create a new `Car` object, our initializer function could "refill" the tank and set the car mileage to zero right after that object is created. Initializers are more advanced than other function types, so they'll be discussed in more detail later.

Subclasses and Casting

Subclasses

We can define **subclasses** in classes. Subclasses inherit all of the attributes and functions of the parent class but can also override inherited functions/attributes or add new ones.

To visualize how classes and subclasses work together, think of the class `Automobile` as the "parent" for the `Car` class. In this sense, a `Car` inherits all of the attributes of an `Automobile`. Then, under the `Car` class, we can define two subclasses: `Coupe` and `Sedan`. Each of these `Coupe` and `Sedan` classes will have the attributes and functions of a basic `Car`, in addition to its own functions and attributes. It will also have attributes and functions from the `Automobile` class as it is indirectly a subclass of `Automobile`.

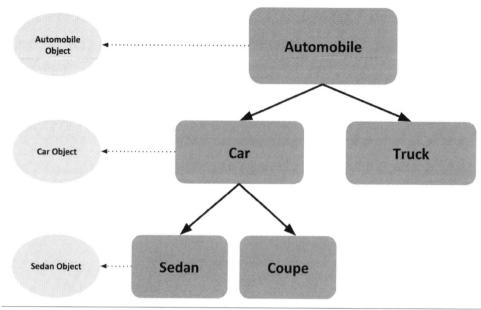

Figure 7-1

In this class hierarchy, Automobile is the superclass of the Car and Truck classes. We can either create a more general Automobile object from the superclass, or we can create a Car object from the subclass Car. The Car object is in fact both an Automobile and and a Car.

The same applies for the Car class, which is not only a subclass of Automobile, but also a superclass of the Sedan and Coupe classes.

This is one of the key advantages of OOP. Because of the ability to create subclasses, we can categorize items efficiently, creating layers of categories. For instance, the Alert Controller class we created in the previous chapter is a subclass of the View Controller class. That's why we were able to plug it into the present() function, which accepts View Controllers as a parameter. Inherently, the Alert Controller is a type of View Controller, just as a sedan is a type of car and a car is a type of automobile.

Casting

This segues perfectly into the next concept: type/class casting. **Casting** is the conversion of one type of object to another related object. We have used casting in our apps already. Although the conversion from String to Int in Swift works a little bit differently than regular casting, casting, at its core, is still converting one type to another.

For instance, if we wanted to convert an explicit Sedan object to a Car, we can do so by casting the Sedan type to be a Car type, as the object already has attributes and functions of both objects (since a Sedan is a Car).

However, if we wanted to cast a Car to a Sedan (the other way around), we cannot do so, because the Sedan is a subclass. Subclasses can and usually do contain attributes and functions that their parent classes do not. Thus, if we attempted to turn a car into a sedan using a cast, it would fail because a Car may not have all of the attirubtes and functions that a Sedan does.

The simple rule is that we can only cast from a certain class to another class if the cast is converting to a more generic class (casting can only happen up the hierarchy in *Figure 7-1*).

There are ways to overcome this, however. Using initializing functions or other methods that we'll learn in this section, we can create new subclass objects from superclass objects. Instead of truly casting, however, this is transferring the superclass functions and attributes to the subclass and filling in the extra pieces that subclasses have.

So even though we commonly use the word "casting" to describe the conversion of an Integer to a String, it's really just an initializing function that reads in the Integer and runs code to represent that Integer in a String form.

Chapter Summary

If most of this still seems relatively abstract, it's because it is. This chapter served as a high-level, conceptual introduction into the concepts that we'll cover in this section. For now, make sure to understand the key components of Object-Oriented Programming, and we'll look at the specifics in the next chapters, starting with classes and then functions.

End-of-Chapter Exercises

1) Swift is the only main programming language that uses Object-Oriented Programming.

(A) True

(B) False

(2) In Swift, _____ serve as the "blueprint" for _____.

(A) attributes, classes

(B) classes, attributes

(C) objects, classes

(D) classes, objects

(3) A Car object's color is an example of a(n):

(A) class

(B) object

(C) attribute

(D) function

(4) A Car object's speedUp( ) is an example of a(n):

(A) class

(B) object

(C) attribute

(D) function

(5) All functions must have input parameters.

(A) True

(B) False

(6) All functions must have output return values.

(A) True

(B) False

(7) Assume a class `Tiger` has superclass `Animal` and subclass `Siberian`. A `Tiger` object can be cast as:

(A) Both an `Animal` and a `Siberian`

(B) Only a `Siberian`

(C) Only an `Animal`

(D) None of the above

(8) I'm ready to start learning Object-Oriented concepts!

(A) True

(B) True

Answers

1. B
2. D
3. C
4. D
5. B
6. B
7. C
8. A,B

Answer Explanations

1) **(B)** Many other languages, such as Java and C#, use OOP.

2) **(D)** In Swift, classes are the "blueprints" for objects.

3) **(C)** A color is a property of an object, so it is an attribute.

4) **(D)** speedUp() is an action of an object, so it is a function.

5) **(B)** Parameters are optional for functions and depend entirely on the objective of the function.

6) **(B)** Return values are optional for functions and depend entirely on the objective of the function.

7) **(C)** A class cannot be cast as one of its subclasses. However, it can be cast as its superclass.

8) **(A,B)** :)

Chapter Eight: Classes (OOP)

Introduction

It's time to learn the in-depth concepts of Object-Oriented Programming. The most fundamental Object-Oriented structure is the *class*. As we learned in the previous chapter, classes are frameworks/templates for objects that created while coding. Let's continue using the "car" analogy to demonstrate how classes are created and used.

We will be using Swift Playgrounds. Open up a new, blank Playground titled `Classes`, and let's get started!

Usage of Classes

Everything in Swift and other OOP languages <u>must</u> all be contained within some sort of class. If code is written outside of a class, it has no way of being accessed or run, leaving it useless.

This is why everything we ran in our first two apps was contained in a class called `ViewController`. The `ViewController` class was created to be a template/blueprint for the View Controller structure we created on the Storyboard. The class outlined the steps and coded the functionality of that specific structure. You can see how all of the code (with the exception of `import` statements and a few comments) was defined in the `ViewController` class:

```
1   //
2   //  ViewController.swift
3   //  My Very First App
4   //
5   //  Created by Etash Kalra
6   //  Copyright © Etash Kalra. All rights reserved.
7   //
8
9   import UIKit

11  class ViewController: UIViewController {
12
    @IBOutlet weak var numberOneTF: UITextField!
    @IBOutlet weak var numberTwoTF: UITextField!
    @IBOutlet weak var answerLabel: UILabel!
16
    @IBAction func addClicked(_ sender: Any) {
18
19      let firstNumber = Int(numberOneTF.text!)
20      let secondNumber = Int(numberTwoTF.text!)
21
22      let sum = firstNumber! + secondNumber!
23      answerLabel.text = String(sum)
24  }
25
    @IBAction func subtractClicked(_ sender: Any) {
27
28      let firstNumber = Int(numberOneTF.text!)
29      let secondNumber = Int(numberTwoTF.text!)
30
31      let difference = firstNumber! - secondNumber!
32      answerLabel.text = String(difference)
33
34  }
35
36  override func viewDidLoad() {
37      super.viewDidLoad()
38      // Do any additional setup after loading the view, typically from a nib.
39  }
40
41  override func didReceiveMemoryWarning() {
42      super.didReceiveMemoryWarning()
43      // Dispose of any resources that can be recreated.
44  }
45
46
47  }
```

Class

Figure 8-1

When we create or access new files in the Xcode Project editor (such as the default ViewController file), Swift automatically creates classes in those files to make the editor easier to use. However, often times we will either need to create our own custom classes or we will need to use some of the advanced features in a class. This chapter will help in understanding the programming techniques and features of classes in Swift.

Creating Classes

First, let's learn how to create a class. Creating a basic class is a simple task. Simply type the keyword class, followed by the name of the class and opening and closing braces.

In class naming conventions, we use UpperCamelCase, which is similar to camelCase in which all words are joined together into one long identifier, and the first letter of each word (including the first word) is capitalized.

To create a basic `Car` class, write the following code on the Playground:

```
1   class Car {
2           //inside the class
3   }
```

In a class, we can create functions, attribute variables, or other items. We'll look more at functions in the following chapter, but let's create some attributes in this class.

Remember variables can fall into two categories: constants and regular (dynamic) variables. Similarly, we can create constant or dynamic attribute variables in an object. For instance, we can define a constant variable `wheels` for a car, and set it equal to 4, as we want all of our `Car` objects to have only 4 `wheels`:

```
1   class Car {
2           let wheels = 4
3   }
```

 Remember to indent each line inside the class by one indent! Anything within braces in Swift should be one more tab inside than the alignment at which the opening and closing braces are.

We can also create regular variables (such as the speed of a car) in a class. Even though each `Car` object we create can have different values for its `speed`, in order for `speed` to be an attribute, we have to set an initial default value inside the class definition:

```
1   class Car {
2           let wheels = 4
3           var speed = 0
4   }
```

After we define the "blueprint" for how a `Car` object should act, we can initialize the class/blueprint as an object. To create a new object from a class, we just need to initialize a new variable, and set its value equal to the expression `Car()`. The parentheses indicate that we are creating a **new** object from the `Car` class:

```
8   var MyCar = Car()
```

 The initialization of the new `Car` object called `MyCar` occurs outside of the class. Playgrounds work differently than normal Xcode Projects, so it is fine that the `MyCar` initialization statement is not in another class.

Now, in the MyCar object, we can access the object's <u>default</u> attributes. Let's print these attributes. To access an object's attributes, enter the name of the object (not the general class name) and add a dot (.) followed by the name of the attribute that you want to access.

Thus, the speed attribute in the MyCar object can be accessed via MyCar.speed and can be printed like other variables:

```
9    var MyCar = Car()
10   print(MyCar.speed)
```

 Note that we used the **object name** (MyCar) not the **class name** (Car) when retrieving attributes for the MyCar object.

Because the value of speed in MyCar is initially the default value we defined in the Car class, the code above will print out 0 in the console.

We can change the value of the speed attribute in the MyCar class because it is a non-constant (dynamic) variable. This is done by setting the attribute (MyCar.speed) equal to a valid value, like 60:

```
12   MyCar.speed = 60
```

Now, if we print MyCar.speed, we will see that the value has changed to 60:

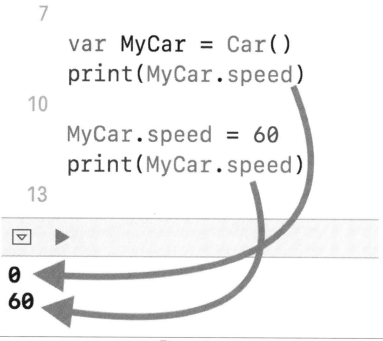

Figure 8-2

However, if we try to change the wheels attribute in the MyCar object, we cannot, because the Car class defined wheels as a **constant** variable (unchangeable).

Subclasses

We briefly touched on subclasses in the previous chapter. To define a subclass, recall the Automobile/Car/Sedan analogy. A general Automobile class can have a more specific subclass Car, which can have a more specific subclass Sedan. Each subclass inherits attributes and functions from its parents class and adds its own attributes and functions.

To demonstrate how subclasses work, we will modify the Car class. Instead of deleting the Car class we have right now, comment out all of the existing code on the Playground. To comment blocks of code out without manually commenting each line with //, either use the multi-line comment feature or select the code using the cursor and press the Command and / keys.

```
          ⊞  <  >  ⇥ Classes
   1  //class Car {
   2  //
   3  //        let wheels = 4
   4  //        var speed = 0
   5  //
   6  //}
   7  //
   8  //var MyCar = Car()
   9  //print(MyCar.speed)
  10  //
  11  //MyCar.speed = 60
  12  //print(MyCar.speed)
```

Figure 8-3

Now, let's first create a general Automobile superclass, which will be the blueprint for all objects that are either Automobiles or objects of a subclass, such as Car (we'll create a Car class in a bit).

Start by defining the class as you would any class:

```
14    class Automobile {
15            //
16    }
```

In this class, put default values for all of the attributes an automobile has, regardless of its specific classification. In our example, all `Automobile` objects will have the variables `name` (String), `wheels` (Integer), `speed` (Float), `parked` (Boolean). Each of these will be a regular variable (*not* a constant).

Go ahead and define each of these variables in the `Automobile` class with default values:

```
14    class Automobile {
15            var name = "Car"
16            var wheels = 0
17            var speed = 0.0
18            var parked = true
19    }
```

Now, we have a general class `Automobile`, which can either be the blueprint for a physical object that we **instantiate** from the class or serve as a superclass.

Instantiation

Instantiation refers to the creation of an object from a class. When we create an object from the class (blueprint), we are create a "physical" **instance** of the class.

Because we have already dealt with instantiating an object from a class in the old `Car` class example, we will continue by creating a subclass of `Automobile`.

Let's create a new `Car` class which is not an independent class, but rather an inheriting subclass of `Automobile`. To define a subclass, define a class as you normally would and add a colon (:) and the name of the superclass to the heading:

```
21    class Car: Automobile {
22            //
23    }
```

Now, in the `Car` subclass, we automatically have the default attributes `name`, `wheels`, `speed`, and `parked`. Even though we cannot see the direct definition of these variables in the `Car` class, they are inherited from the parent class `Automobile`.

We can add additional values to the `Car` class which would not exist in the parent class. For instance, let's add another variable called `transmission` (either `"Gas"`, `"Electric"`, or `"Hybrid"`) to the `Car` class. This attribute would be available for all `Car` instances, but not any `Automobile` instances, even though all `Automobile` attributes are available in the child `Car` class. Try adding the `transmission` variable as a String:

```
21    class Car: Automobile {
22            var transmission = "Electric"
23    }
```

In addition to adding new attributes to a child class, we can override the default values of attributes from the parent class. For example, we will override the default value of wheels to be 4 in the Car class.

To override the wheels attribute, which is defined in the parent class, we will need an override init() function in the Car class:

```
21    class Car: Automobile {
22            var transmission = "Electric"
23            override init() {
24                    //
25            }
26    }
```

We will go into more depth about functions (specifically the init() function) in the following chapter. For now, know that the init() function is a default function (initializer) that is automatically called every time an object is instantiated from a class. We are going to attempt to override this default function to change the default value of wheels from 0 to 4 in the Car class. Remember that the default value of wheels was defined in the parent (Automobile) class as 0, which gets passed down as the default to its child class Car.

In the init() function, we first must ensure that we are initializing a class correctly by calling the init() function from the superclass first and then changing the values that we want to. If we do not initialize the superclass when an object is created, the Car class will not be able to receive any inherited properties from the Automobile class.

The first line of our new function should be calling the superclass initialization function. Add the following line to the init() function for Car:

```
24            super.init()
```

Now, we can change the default values for attributes, such as wheels. For a Car object to change its inherited values, the initialized object will need to reference itself with the keyword self. When a Car object is created, the init() function will change its own (self) value of wheels to 4:

```
21  class Car: Automobile {
22      var transmission = "Electric"
23      override init() {
24          super.init()
25          self.wheels = 4
26      }
27  }
```

We have just overridden the default value for wheels in the child class in addition to adding an attribute called transmission. Both of these items were done at the same time as inheriting attributes from the parent class.

To verify, let's initialize/instantiate a new Car object:

```
29  var MyCar = Car()
```

In the object, print all of the following values:

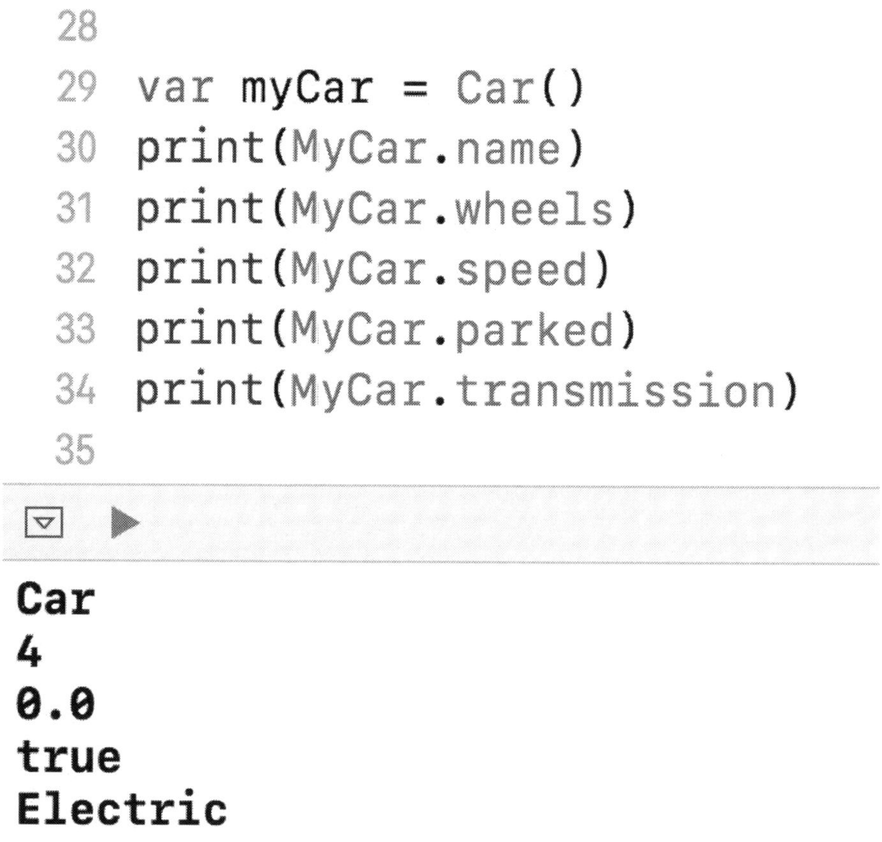

```
28
29  var myCar = Car()
30  print(MyCar.name)
31  print(MyCar.wheels)
32  print(MyCar.speed)
33  print(MyCar.parked)
34  print(MyCar.transmission)
35
```

```
▽  ▶
```

```
Car
4
0.0
true
Electric
```

Figure 8-4

Notice that even though name, speed, and parking were not explicitly defined in the Car class, they were inherited from Automobile. Additionally, we can access transmission and the value of wheels has been updated.

Much of subclasses revolves around the inheritance of properties and functions. In this short section, we have covered how basic properties can be passed on through subclasses, and, in the next chapter, we will look more at the subclassing of functions and the use of init() in superclasses and subclasses.

Reference Types

Another key aspect of classes is that objects are reference types. Each object created has a certain reference key (think of it as a "location" where the object is stored in the memory of the program). When setting a variable equal to an object, comparing two objects, or passing an object through a function, Swift only passes this reference key. Other types, such as Strings or Integers, however, are not reference types: when they are compared or passed, only their value is taken into account.

For instance, say we have two Integer variables, a and b that we defined separately. If we set both of these variables equal to 100, then the expression (a == b) will evaluate to true.

However, imagine that we initialize two separate Car objects, CarA and CarB, and set all of their parameters to be the same. Even if these two objects have identical values, the expression (CarA == CarB) will evaluate to false. The reason for this inequality is that Swift compares objects as Reference Types. Instead of checking the properties of both objects, Swift checks the unique reference key of each of these objects. Because these two objects do not reference the same object (CarA is inherently identical but separate from CarB), the expression is false.

Another example that proves objects are reference types can be shown by what happens when we set two variables equal to the same object. Changing one of the variables changes the other as well because they both have the same reference key. Here's what I mean:

We already have a MyCar object stored as a variable. Underneath this declaration, create another variable called MyCar2 and set it equal to MyCar:

```
29   var MyCar = Car()
30   var MyCar2 = MyCar
```

Now, if we print the .name of both of these cars, they have the same default value:

```
31   print MyCar.name // prints "Car"
32   print MyCar2.name // prints "Car"
```

Following this, change the name of MyCar to be "Ferrari":

```
34   MyCar.name = "Ferrari"
```

Now, print the .name values of MyCar and MyCar2 again. Even though we only changed the name of MyCar, the MyCar2.name value **also** changed to "Ferrari":

```
36   print MyCar.name // prints "Ferrari"
37   print MyCar2.name // prints "Ferrari"
```

Likewise, if we change the speed attribute to 100 on MyCar2, MyCar's speed also becomes 100, since they're actually set to be the same object:

```
39   MyCar2.speed = 100
40   print(MyCar.speed) // prints 100
```

The reason for this is that MyCar and MyCar2 are two different variables **referencing** the same object. When you change the value of one object, both of the reference points see the change, because they are viewing the same singular object with the same reference key. This reference key was what was passed when we said MyCar2 = MyCar. If we had set these two variables equal to a value type such as Int or String, and then set them equal to each other, they would have the same value. However, changing one of the value type variables would not affect the other variable's value.

This proves that objects are reference types, rather than value types, like Ints. This is a fundamental aspect of classes that you'll need to know to continue Swift programming, as well as in any other Object-Oriented programming language.

Chapter Summary

We've learned quite a lot in this chapter! With classes being the most fundamental structure in Swift and other OOP languages, we will see them quite often. In addition to storing values and passing along attributes and functions, classes can also take in parameters, run functions, and much more. In the next chapter, we will go even further into object-oriented programming by throwing functions into the mix. Functions are inherently dependent on their parent class (just as everything else in Swift is), so classes and objects will be used quite a bit in the upcoming chapters.

To recap what we went over in this chapter:

- Everything we program on an app **must** be within a class (Playgrounds are an exception)
- Classes are the "blueprints" for objects
- Objects can be created and assigned to a variable
- Classes have attributes and functions defined within them
- An object's attributes can only be accessed after it is instantiated
- Classes can inherit traits from other parent classes (subclassing)
- Classes can override inherited values
- Objects are **reference types**, whereas `String`, `Int`, and other variable types are value types

Great job so far! Once we become more comfortable with these Object-Oriented concepts in the next few chapters of this section, we will be well on our way to creating even more functional apps. In the next chapter, we get into the more advanced parts of OOP, mainly dealing with functions.

End-of-Chapter Exercises

1) `Import` statements must be defined within a class:

(A) True

(B) False

2) Which of the following is a correct way of writing a class definition?

(A)
```
class MyClass [
      // class
   ]
```

(B)
```
class MyClass : (
      // class
   )
```

(C)
```
class MyClass (
      // class
   )
```

(D)
```
class MyClass {
      // class
   }
```


3) Given an object `MyCar` of class `Car`, how would we access its `speed` attribute?

(A) `MyCar:speed`

(B) `Car:speed`

(C) `MyCar.speed`

(D) `Car.speed`

4) Which of the following is a correct way of writing a subclass definition?

```
(A) class MyClass: superClass {
        // super class
    }
```

```
(B) class MyClass : superClass (
        // class
    )
```

```
(C) subclass MyClass : superClass (
        // class
    )
```

```
(D) subclass MyClass: superClass {
        // class
    }
```

5) Which of the following is a correct way of overwriting default values from a superclass?

```
(A) override init() {
        super.init()
    }
```

```
(B) override init() {
    }
```

```
(C) init() override {
    }
```

```
(D) init() {
        super.init()
    }
```

6) Given the following code:

```
let Bike1 = Bike()
let Bike2 = Bike()
let Bike3 = Bike1
let Bike4 = Bike()
let Bike2 = Bike3
```

Which of the following variables refer to the same Bike object?

(A) Bike1, Bike3

(B) Bike1, Bike4

(C) Bike1, Bike2, Bike 3

(D) All of the variables refer to the same Bike object.

Answers

1. **B**
2. **D**
3. **C**
4. **A**
5. **A**
6. **C**

Answer Explanations

1) **(B)** All `import` statements should be defined outside of a class.

2) **(D)** Classes are enclosed in curly braces.

3) **(C)** An attribute of an <u>object</u> can be accessed by typing the <u>object name</u>, followed by a period and the attribute name.

4) **(A)** Subclasses are still defined using the keyword `class`, and are enclosed in curly braces.

5) **(A)** Overwriting default values from a super class should use the `init()` function specified with the `override` keyword. Additionally, such functions should also call `super.init()` to instantiate the superclass prior to changing any values.

6) **(C)** After the first two lines, `Bike1` and `Bike2` start as two separate objects. On line three, `Bike3` is instantiated and refers to the same object as `Bike1`. On line four, `Bike4` is instantiated as a separate object from the rest. On line five, `Bike2` refers to the same object as `Bike3`, which refers to the same object as `Bike1`. Therefore, `Bike1`, `Bike2`, and `Bike3` all refer to the same object.

Chapter Nine: Functions (OOP)

Introduction

In addition to classes, functions are a fundamental part of **Object-Oriented Programming (OOP)**. Functions are defined segments of code, which can receive an input and return an output. Whenever a function is called, or accessed, the code inside the function is run with an input value that may have been passed in. In **any** program or app we create, functions are absolutely necessary. They enable functionality of the applications you create and must be defined in classes. In this chapter, we will take a good look at how to use functions and see how they fit within the world of OOP and Swift.

For this chapter, we will be using Swift Playground again! Open a new Playground file called `Functions` to get started.

Why Functions?

While programming in most modern languages, especially while developing apps, we need a way to perform specific tasks at certain times. For instance, when a user presses a button, we would like for our program to respond by performing a certain set of actions. Often times, we will also have sets of actions which we would like to repeatedly perform. Functions can be called repeatedly so that those sets of actions are run multiple times. Without functions, programs would be run on a single-file, from line one to the end. Though some programs may use this type of functionality, it allows for very little variability in our code. In addition, without functions, our code would be repetitive and not allow for much user interaction. To eliminate these issues of non-reusable and static code, Object-Oriented Programming uses functions.

Functions allow for code to be organized and reusable, as well as allow for us to perform different actions depending on what, where, and how the user interacts with our application. They also allows us to pass parameter values (remember these from Chapter 7?) within sets of statements to allow for a range of a possibilities within our programs and apps.

 If you don't remember what parameters and return values are, make sure to review these concepts in Chapter 7!

There are two places where functions are visible. These two areas are similar to how classes and objects are seen in OOP.

The first place is the **definition** of the function. Just as we blueprint how a class will behave, we must define how a function will act. The definition itself does not run any of the code inside it. It only tells the compiler what to do when we access that function. It's just like a class: the class "blueprint" was not an object itself, but it defined how an object will be built.

The second part is the **function call**, where we tell the compiler to run the set of statements within the function. In a function call, we can both pass in input values and receive output values.

Defining Functions, Parameters, and Return Values

In Swift, functions are defined using the `func` keyword, followed by the name of the function (without spaces). Functions, like variable types, are named using lowerCamelCase. Following the name, put a pair of parentheses ( ), which will contain the parameters of the function. If there are no parameters, leave the parentheses empty. And of course, like loops and classes, functions encapsulate statements with a pair of curly braces { }.

Additionally, if the function has a return value, we will define that return type by using an "arrow" (-> dash and angle bracket). This arrow is defined in the header (before the opening curly brace) and is followed by the type of value the function should return.

Too many components? Let's break down the definition of a function to see how it works:

```
1    func functionName(parameters...) -> returnType {
2            //
3    }
```

A function needs needs 5 components to be defined:

1. `func` keyword
2. Function Name (lowerCamelCase)
3. Parentheses (with or without parameters)
4. An optional return type
5. Pair of curly braces { }

Let's start by defining a simple `isEven()` function in our Playground file. The function will take a number and output whether the number is even. Therefore, this function will have one parameter of `Int` type and a return value of `Bool` type. In this function, we will output `true` if the inputted number is even and `false` if it is not (if it is odd).

Let's define this function. Starting with the easiest parts (excluding parameters and return types), write the following:

```
1  func isEven() {
2    //
3  }
```

A function that has **no** parameters or return values would have the structure above. However, our isEven() function has both a parameter and a return value, so we'll need to define those. Define the parameter within the parentheses by giving the parameter a name (let's call it num), followed by a colon and the parameter type (Int):

```
1  func isEven(num: Int) {
2    //
3  }
```

Finally, add the "return arrow" (->) followed by the return type (Bool):

```
1  func isEven(num: Int) -> Bool {
2    //
3  }
```

 While typing this function header into the Playground compiler, you may encounter an error: Missing return in a function expected to return 'Bool'. Because we declared this function will return a Bool value, but it does not return anything yet, the compiler is alerting us. Ignore this for now, as we will define the return statement in just a moment.

Now, let's look at the body of this function. Before starting, ask yourself the following question:

 In this function, we must determine whether num is odd or even and then return true or false accordingly. Which structure will we need to use to handle this task?

Think back to the programming flow structures that we have learned (for loops, while loops, if/else statements). Our code will be executed in a different manner for two different possibilities (even or odd), so we will need a conditional statement to represent the two possibilities. Thus, our use of a conditional statement rules out for loops, which are not based on conditional statements such as the one we need. Additionally, our code will only need to assess the condition once, as num is an unchanging number within our function. Thus, while loops are ruled out as well.

We must use an if structure to classify our number as odd or even. However, we will be returning a Bool value regardless of whether num is odd or even, so we will need an if else structure to handle each possibility.

To write the first `if` statement, use the modulus operator (%). Remember that this operator is used on two numbers (a % b) and returns the remainder of the first number divided by the second.

The expression num % 2 for any number can only evaluate to zero or one. If the number is even, then it is divisible by two (remainder is zero). If it is odd, then it has a remainder of one when divided by two. Thus, we can have a conditional statement using modulus to detect if num is even. We can use the `else` statement to handle the condition that num is not even (odd).

In the `if` and the `else` blocks, we need to add a `return` statement, which outputs the expression that follows it. Therefore, one of our blocks (the one that handles num being even) should `return true`, and the other should `return false`.

 Try creating this `if else` structure using a conditional statement with a modulus operator, and having the appropriate `return` statement for each block.

The first part of the structure is the `if` block, in which our conditional statement will determine whether num is even. In this conditional statement, check if num % 2 is equal to zero:

```
1   func isEven(num: Int) -> Bool {
2       if num % 2 == 0 {
3
4       }
5   }
```

We also need an `else` statement. If the `if` condition fails, then we know num is an odd number.

```
1   func isEven(num: Int) -> Bool {
2       if num % 2 == 0 {
3
4       } else {
5
6       }
7   }
```

Finally, add the `return` statements to the respective blocks. Because the function is called `isEven()`, we should `return true` in the first block:

```
1  func isEven(num: Int) -> Bool {
2     if num % 2 == 0 {
3        return true
4     } else {
5        return false
6     }
7  }
```

Calling Functions

Now that we have defined our function and it is able to receive input values (parameters) and output values (return values), we are ready to access our function with an actual number passed as num.

Calling a function is relatively easy. Type the name of the function and pass parameter values in the pair of parentheses that follow the name call. We can also print the result of a function:

```
9  print( isEven(num: 5) ) // false is printed
```

Remember that functions also have a scope, meaning that they can only be called from certain areas. All of our functions will exist in a class, so we can only access them from other functions within the class. If we want to access a function from outside its class, we must initialize an object from the class, which will allow for the function to accessible through the initialized object.

To demonstrate, we are going to create a class around the isEven() function. We will call this class Number:

```
1  class Number {
2     func isEven(num: Int) -> Bool {
3        if num % 2 == 0 {
4           return true
5        } else {
6           return false
7        }
8     }
9  }
```

Remember to indent all of the code within the class after creating it around our function!

Now, if we run our Playground file with the print(isEven(5)) statement, the Playground will not run the function because it does not have access to a function in an uninitialized class. isEven() can only be called from another function within the class or from an initialized Number object. Thus, we will have to instantiate a Number object to access the function. To access a function from object, we do just as we did with variables: attach a period (.) after the object name and then add the function name. Let's try creating the object and calling the function from the object:

```
11  var numberObject = Number()
12  print( numberObject.isEven(num: 5) )
```

We get the correct result now! We had to instantiate the class to access the function because functions often access attributes that are internal to an object.

Initializers

In addition to having "regular" functions contained within them, classes also have special types of functions called **initializers**. We worked with these types of functions briefly in the previous chapter, when we wanted to override default values for attributes from a superclass.

Initializer functions are functions in classes that are always run whenever an object of a class is initialized. Whenever we set default values within a class, as we did in the Car class in the previous chapter, those default values are set whenever our object is created. If we set a default value for each of our attributes, then Swift provides a default initializer function to handle the creation of the object and the assignment of values to the variables.

However, classes can also have parameterized initialization, meaning that we can pass input values to an object while creating it. These input values can be used to assign default values. We may also want to override inherited characteristics from a superclass. Both of these scenarios are common motivations for creating an initializer function (rather than using the default one that Swift runs).

To begin, we will look at parametrized initialization, which is used to create an object with parameters. Let's change our Number class so that it has an Int attribute called value. However, we will only specify that the attribute must be of type Int and not add a default value for value:

```
1  class Number {
2      var value: Int
3      ...
4  }
```

Now, let's add an initializer function to the class. This function will take in a parameter and assign the parameter to the value attribute. Initializer functions have the identifier init() without the keyword func:

```
4      init(value: Int) {
5  
6      }
```

If we also name the init() parameter value (in addition to the class attribute value), then when we set the attribute value equal to the parameter value, we will have to specify which is which, as the compiler will not be able to distinguish them. Without specifying, value = value in the body of the function would result in the `value` parameter setting itself equal to itself (does nothing). Thus, to specify that we want to set the class attribute `value` equal to the function parameter `value`, we will use the keyword `self`. This keyword references the class itself, so that the compiler identifies the class attribute `value`, as well as the parameter:

```
1   class Number {
2      var value: Int
3
4      init(value: Int) {
5         self.value = value
6      }
7      ...
8   }
```

We have successfully created the initialization function for the `Number` class. Now, whenever we create a `Number` object, we must pass an integer value for `value`, which becomes the default value for our class. Below the class definition, we had initialized a `numberObject` earlier, without any parameters. However, to make this initialization work, we must conform to the initialization function by passing a parameter value into the object's initialization, as on Line 17:

```
1   class Number {
2      var value: Int
3
4      init(value: Int) {
5         self.value = value
6      }
7
8      func isEven(num: Int) -> Bool {
9         if num % 2 == 0 {
10           return true
11        } else {
12           return false
13        }
14     }
15  }
16
17  var numberObject = Number(value: 5)
```

We can also create multiple initializers, to allow for objects to be created in different ways. Each initializer we create must take a different set of parameters. Then, when creating an object we can choose from one of several ways to set up the object. Let's create a second initializer function which sets the object `value` to be the additive inverse of the parameter's value. To create the second initializer, use the same `init()` keyword, except with different parameter names or types. This time, we will set the parameter to be an Integer value called `negative`:

```
8     init(negative: Int) {
9
10    }
```

Now, we will set our value attribute equal to the negative of the parameter's value. Using the self keyword is optional for this statement, as negative and value will not be confused by the compiler (it is still recommended to use the self keyword):

```
8     init(negative: Int) {
9         self.value = -negative
10    }
```

These two initializer functions are able to coexist within our class, even if they both have the same name.

Try creating another object called anotherNumber and pass in the parameter negative: 5. After printing the value of this object and our first numberObject, we can see that both initializers work. The initializer the compiler uses is based on the parameters you pass while creating the object.

```
1   class Number {
2       var value: Int
3
4       init(value: Int) {
5           self.value = value
6       }
7
8       init(negative: Int) {
9           self.value = -negative
10      }
11
12      func isEven(num: Int) -> Bool {
13          if num % 2 == 0 {
14              return true
15          } else {
16              return false
17          }
18      }
19  }
20
21  var numberObject = Number(value: 5)
22  print numberObject.value // prints 5
23
24  var anotherNumber = Number(negative: 5)
25  print anotherNumber.value // prints -5
```

In addition to creating initializers to set default values and attributes for an object, these special functions have a wide range of abilities, including calling other functions, accessing superclasses, and running other blocks of code. Many of these possibilities will be explored in more advanced detail as we create apps. For now, let's review how we can interact with a superclass's initializers.

Recall the code we wrote in the last chapter:

```
14   class Automobile {
15           var name = "Car"
16           var wheels = 0
17           var speed = 0.0
18           var parked = true
19   }
20
21   class Car: Automobile {
22           var transmission - "Electric"
23           override init() {
24                   super.init()
25                   self.wheels = 4
26           }
27   }
```

On Line 23, we create an initializer function. Not only does this initializer function replace the (hidden) default initializer function for the Car class, but it also replaces the default initializer for the Automobile superclass. Though we are overriding and providing a default initializer for the Car, we **must** also provide some sort of initializer for its superclass, Automobile. Thus, we must call the default superclass initializer with the super.init() function call on Line 24. The super keyword refers to the superclass instance of the Car object (as a Car object is both a Car **and** an Automobile). Without the call to the super initializer, Automobile would not properly initialize as the superclass for Car, thus causing an error.

Simple take: whenever overriding an initializer in a class that has a superclass associated with it, **always** (almost without exception) call super.init().

Chapter Summary

You are almost done with the fundamentals of Object-Oriented Programming in Swfit! Some of the functions you'll see in the future will be auto-generated, but we will also create many of our own functions to complete tasks. In addition to having parameters, return types, and initializers, functions can also have nested functions, multiple parameters (and return values), variadic parameters, in/out parameters, and optional return types. In the next chapter, we will wrap up the basics of Object-Oriented Programming by piecing all of the concepts together, while learning about optional types and diving into the scope of variables/functions. I hope this chapter was a much deeper rundown of how functions work, and you'll get even more advanced with them as we start creating apps at the end of this section and onwards.

Recapping everything covered in this chapter:

- Swift functions have two parts: defining functions and calling functions.
- Functions are defined using the `func` keyword.
- Functions can contain parameters or return types, which are defined in the function header.
- The content of a function is contained within curly braces { } similar to loops, if-statements, and classes.
- Functions can be called by typing the function name followed by parentheses containing any required parameters.
- Function calls run the contained code with defined parameters and evaluate to their return value.
- All classes have an initializer function, which can be overridden using the keyword `init`.
- The `self` keyword can be used to differentiate class attributes from local parameters in a function.
- Classes can have multiple initializers.
- When overriding an initializer of a class with a superclass, the superclass initializer must be called with `super.init()`.

End-of-Chapter Exercises

1) Which of the following naming conventions do Swift functions use?

(A) lowerCamelCase

(B) UpperCamelCase

(C) lowercase

(D) snake_case

2) Which of the following is **not** a valid way of writing a function definition?

```
(A) func functionName(param1: Int) {
        // function
    }
```

```
(B) func functionName(param1: Int) -> String {
        // function
    }
```

```
(C) func functionName -> String {
        // function
    }
```

```
(D) func functionName() -> String {
        // function
    }
```

3) Will the following code throw an error? Why or why not?

```
func myFunction(number: Int) -> Bool {
        for i in 1...number {
                print(i)
        }
}
```

(A) **No**, there is nothing wrong with the code.

(B) **Yes**, the parameter in the function header was defined incorrectly.

(C) **Yes**, there is no return value in the body of the function.

(D) None of the above.

4) The expression 17 % 5 will evaluate to:

(A) 2

(B) 12

(C) 3

(D) 0

5) Which of the following is a valid function call?

```
(A)  func functionName(num: 12)
```

```
(B)  func functionName(num: Int: 12)
```

```
(C)  functionName(num: 12) -> String
```

```
(D)  functionName(num: 12)
```

6) Given object `MyObject` has a function named `myFunction` with return type `String` and no input parameters, which of the following is a valid function call?

(A) `MyObject.myFunction() -> String`

(B) `MyObject.myFunction()`

(C) `MyObject[myFunction(String)]`

(D) `MyObject[myFunction()]`

7) Which of the following is a valid initializer function?

(A)
```
func init() {
      // function
   }
```

(B)
```
func init {
      // function
   }
```

(C)
```
init() {
      // function
   }
```

(D)
```
init {
      // function
   }
```

8) Given the following class, what will be the output if `MyNumber.show(value: 4)` is run?

```
class Number {
        value = 3

        func show(value: Int) {
                print(value)
                print(self.value)
        }
}
```

(A) 3 4

(B) 4 3

(C) 3 3

(D) 4 4

Answers

1. **A**
2. **C**
3. **C**
4. **A**
5. **D**
6. **B**
7. **C**
8. **B**

Answer Explanations

1) **(A)** Everything in Swift is named uses some variation of camelCase. Functions use lowerCamelCase and classes use UpperCamelCase.

2) **(C)** C is incorrect since all functions must have a pair of parentheses following their function name (even if they have no parameters).

3) **(C)** If a function specifies a return value in its heading, it <u>must</u> return a value before the function completes.

4) **(A)** 17 mod 5 is the equivalent to the remainder when 17 is divided by 5. 17 divided by 5 is 3 with a remainder of 2, thus 17 mod 5 is 2.

5) **(D)** Function namecalls do not use the keyword `func` (only definitions), thus A and B are incorrect. C is incorrect since function calls should not define any return values.

6) **(B)** A function of an object can be called by typing the object's name, followed by a period and then the name of the function.

7) **(C)** Initializer functions do not require the `func` keyword, but still require a pair of parentheses after `init` like all functions.

8) **(B)** When `MyNumber.show(value: 4)` is run, the `value` parameter local to the `show()` function is 4 whereas the `value` attribute for the class is 3. When `print(value)` is called in the `show()` function, `value` references the `value` with the most-local scope, which the `value` parameter, which has value 4. On the next line, when `print(self.value)` is called, `self.value` references the `value` attribute of the class, which is 3. Thus, 4 and then 3 are printed.

Chapter Ten: Scope, Optionals, and Core Concepts

Introduction

As we come to a close on learning the fundamentals of Object-Oriented Programming, this chapter will demonstrate a few final concepts, specifically variable scope and optional types, to aid you in your programming journey. These will undoubtedly be necessary while using Object-Oriented Programming in Swift. In the final part of this chapter, we will discuss core Object-Oriented Programming concepts on a high level. You have already experienced these concepts in action, but we haven't given these concepts a specific name and tied them into the larger realm of computer science yet. The (largely universal) concepts we'll recap are abstraction, encapsulation, inheritance, and polymorphism.

In this chapter, optional types are the only Swift-specific concept that we'll learn. Not every OOP language, and not very many other programming languages in general, use optional types. Scope and our other core concepts (abstraction/encapsulation/inheritance/polymorphism), however, are applicable to all Object-Oriented Languages, from Java to C++.

Variable and Object Scope

Lifetime

In Swift, OOP languages, and much of computer science, there is a fundamental idea of **lifetime**. Lifetime is the period of time for which a certain item, variable, or object is available in a program's memory. Any item in Swift goes through three main phases.

First, the item is declared, at which point it is put into the program's memory. Second, the item lives within the memory for a certain period of time (the lifetime of the item), where it is accessed from its memory location. Third, the item is eventually de-initialized and removed from memory at the end of its lifetime.

Scope and Hierarchy

The lifetime of an item is very closely related to the **scope** of that item.

The scope of the item represents the period of time/amount of code for which the item is **accessible**, whereas the lifetime of an item is the period of time for which the item is **available in memory**.

The scope of any item is dependent on where it was initially declared. The scope of a variable is different if it is declared inside a class, a function, or a control block (if, while, for, etc.). Each of these structures, whether it be a class or a function or a control block, is maintained in a hierarchy. For instance, look at the following sample of code:

```
var item1 = 1
class MyClass {
        var item2 = 2
        func myFunction() {
                var item3 = 3
                for i in 0...10 {
                        var item4 = 4
                }
        }
}
```

In this code, there are four levels of hierarchy. First, there is code that is written outside of MyClass, at the highest level of hierarchy. Below that is code written directly inside MyClass, where item2 is declared. Underneath that is the level of myFunction(), where item3 is declared, and then the fourth level of hierarchy is code written inside the for loop.

 Each level of the hierarchy is distinguished through a "nested" code block (block of code enclosed within curly braces). Code blocks (pairs of curly braces) nested and indented within other code blocks can help distinguish this hierarchy (Global > MyClass > myFunction > for). Each code block starts with a heading, whether it be a class definition, function definition, or loop declaration. Remember to always indent your code properly, with each new code block indented one level in, to allow for this ease in identifying and maintaining hierarchy.

A variable, object, or other item will only be accessible (its scope) to statements on the same or lower level of hierarchy as it. The variable will not be accessible to code in a hierarchical level above where it was declared.

For instance, in the code example above, item1 can be referenced anywhere, as all code is at the same or lower level than the level at which item1 was declared. However, item3 is only accessible to code in myFunction() or below. Statements that try to access item3 from outside myFunction() will not be able to do so, as the scope of that variable is limited to the code block that starts with func myFunction() {...}. However, code written in the for loop **will** be able to access item3, as the for loop is on a level within/under myFunction(). item4, which is declared in the for loop, will not be accessible to myFunction(). The item4 variable is initialized inside the for loop and is removed from memory as soon as the for loop ends, so there is no way a code statement outside the loop can access it.

 Parameters fall on the same level of scope as variables inside of the function. For instance, if myFunction() in the previous example had a parameter, that parameter would be at the **same** scope level as item3.

This difference in scope distinguishes **global** and **local** variables/objects. Relatively, `item1` is the most "global" variable in our example, as it is accessible anywhere because it is not tied to the scope of a class or a code block. However, as we move down our hierarchy, into the class its function(s), our variables become "local." They are no longer globally accessible, but only accessible on a local hierarchical level.

While writing our code, we need to remember where certain variables are accessible, because accessing variables or objects outside of their scope will lead to errors. It's a relatively simple concept, as long as you remember the rule that variables are only accessible within the code block in which they were declared or in "nested" blocks (code blocks that are in the main code block).

 One important thing to note is that even though two items can be at the same level of hierarchy, they are not necessarily both at the same scope. For instance, take the following code with functions `one()` and `two()`:

```
func one() {
  var nameOne = "Jack"
}

func two() {
  var nameTwo = "Jill"
}
```

Even though `nameOne` and `nameTwo` are technically on the same level of hierarchy, they aren't at the same scope, since we cannot access `nameOne` in function `two()` and vice-versa.

Shadowing

It is evident that we can declare objects and variables at different scopes in Swift.

Usually, these items (even at different scopes) will not have the same name, but there are instances in which we will declare two separate items *at different levels of scope* with the same name. Often times, we may need to declare a class attribute with a certain name and declare a function parameter with the same name. Doing so will require the use of two distinct variables. One of these variables will take precedence over the other in places where both variables are in scope. This phenomenon is called **shadowing**, where one of the items will "shadow" the accessibility of the other.

 As a word of caution, notice that we obviously cannot declare two items with the same name at the same level of scope:

```
var myNum = 1
var myNum = 2 // Throws an error
```

However, as we did in the initializer example in Chapter 9, if two variable/object declarations are at different levels of scope, then it is valid for them to have the same name:

```
1   // Try this code out in a Playground file
2   class Hello {
3       var value = 1 // Global declaration
4
5       func something() {
6           var value = 2 // Second declaration with same name
7           print(value)
8       }
9   }
10
11  var hello = Hello() // We have to instantiate the class to use it
12  hello.something()
```

Because one of the two variables above is at a wider-accessible scope than the other, code written outside the function will only be able to access the globally declared `value` variable. But what about code written within the function? Which `value` variable will it access?

The answer is the second declaration. In general, when a code statement has to pick between two different variables with the same name, it will reference the variable with the nearest scope (the most locally accessible variable). Thus, the print statement on Line 7 will print 2, as it is referencing the local declaration of `value` on Line 5.

This is a great demonstration of one variable **shadowing** the other with the same name. Anytime a variable is declared, it takes highest precedence for its name on its level of scope and all nested/lower levels. Any higher scope variables that have the same name are technically still accessible in the program memory, but they are not easily accessed (there are alternate ways to access these variables).

 Note that shadowing is **not** the same as overriding a variable. When we create an instance of a variable that has the same name (but different scope level), both variables still exist. Neither variable influences the other, except that one sometimes takes precedence over the other when accessed on specific levels of scope. To override a variable, we could execute `value = 3`, but, by using the `var` keyword, the compiler initializes a distinct variable with the same name.

To demonstrate, in our class, we can still bypass the preferred local variable to access the global variable. By doing so, we prove that both variables indeed do exist at this scope leve, and that shadowing is **not** overriding a variable.

```
1     ...
2            func something() {
3                    var value = 2 //Second declaration with same name
4                    print(value) //prints 2
5                    print(self.value) //prints 1
6            }
7     ...
```

In our `something()` function, if we use the `self` keyword, it will reference the current `Hello` instance's properties. Thus, because `value` is a class attribute, we can use `self.value` to access it.

Frameworks and Libraries

In most, if not all, of our applications, you will not need to write 100% of the code. The Apple Swift framework and other programming technologies have written preexisting code that we can import into our programs to make coding easier and less redundant. Instead of rewriting long complicated functions and classes, such as `UILabel`, navigation, web access, and notifications, Apple and other frameworks provide **libraries**, which can be accessed using the **import** keyword. Recall we used `import` statements in our first app:

```
8
9    import UIKit
10
11   class ViewController: UIViewController, UITableViewDelegate {
12
```

Figure 10-1

After importing a library such as `UIKit` (outside of our classes), we can utilize the properties of the library. The use of these libraries will be very important in programming our apps.

Optional Types

Another important concept in Swift is **optional types**. Optional types are an outlier in this chapter, as they are not technically part of a traditional object-oriented programming language. However, these types play a huge role in the other OOP and Swift programming concepts. Swift is one of several languages that heavily relies on the use of optional types. Other OOP languages may not rely extensively on optionals, and some do not even have these types.

The `nil` Value

Optional types, often called "optionals," are a property of variables and objects that help solve the problem of non-existing values in variables. Recall the `nil` value we defined as a boolean option in Chapter 4. The `nil` value is not limited to `Boolean` values. It is a valid value for all variable types, including `String` and `Int`. At times, allowing for a variable to have a non-value (`nil` value) is necessary, but, at other times, it can cause issues. For instance, whenever a user has the option of typing into a `UITextField`, the `.value` attribute of the text field can be an empty `String` (`nil`) if the user did not type anything into it. However, if we want to use this `.value` attribute, it needs to contain a value. Handling a situation such as that one requires the use of an optional.

Optional Wrapping

Optional variables are the same as our regular variables, except for one nuance: optional variables allow for `nil` values, whereas regular variables **do not**. An optional type is defined in our code like its regular counterpart but with with a ? (question mark) appended to it. **Int** and **Int?** are two different types, where the latter is an optional type. If you have a variable that is non-optional, like `Int`, you can be certain it will always have some sort of integer value. With the optional type, the variable may have an integer value, but it could also have a `nil` value.

Let's think of *optional* as a wrapper type, such as a gift box which wraps the value of the optional inside of it and can contain something or be empty.

`var myNum: Int? = 2` and **`var myNum: Int? = nil`** are valid definitions of optional values, whereas **`var myNum: Int = nil`** would be invalid since it was not defined as an `Int?` type.

Let's try a small example. Type the following code into a Playground:

```
1   var myString: String? = nil
2
3   if myString == nil {
4           print("nil value")
5   } else {
6           print(myString)
7   }
```

When this code is run, the console will print `nil value`.

Let's change the value of `myString` from `nil` to a non-empty value:

```
1   var myString: String? = "Swift!"
```

After this code is run, the compiler should print `"Swift!"`. Though this is partially true, the playground actually outputs `"Swift!"` in an `Optional()` wrapper:

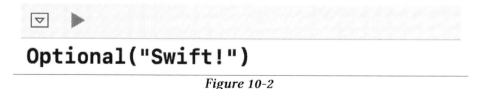

Optional("Swift!")

Figure 10-2

`Optional("Swift"!)` is outputted when we print our `String?` variable because the compiler is **wrapping** our values in an `Optional` wrapper. Remember the "gift box" analogy: because the optional variable has a wrapper around it, there's an extra layer on top of it. The value of an optional variable could be empty, so to communicate the variable type is a `String?` and not a `String`, it has an `Optional` wrapper.

To fix this wrapping issue and get the actual value of the `myString` variable, we can apply a forced unwrapping by adding an exclamation point (`!`) to the end of our variable name call, which removes the `Optional` wrapper:

```
6       print(myString!)
```

This prints `"Swift!"` to the console, without the wrapper.

 Forced unwrapping of an optional variable can be risky. If the "gift box" (optional value) is empty/nil, our app will crash, as unwrapping an empty value is invalid in Swift. As a rule of thumb, always check that an optional variable is not `nil` (as we did) before unwrapping it.

Whenever regular types and optional types interact, the optional types must be unwrapped, as both types must be regular in order to interact. For instance, if we try and add the following, we will get an error:

```
1   var num1: Int? = 1
2   var num2: Int = 2
3
4   print(num1 + num2)
```

In order to correctly execute this code, we have to unwrap `num1`:

```
4   print(num1! + num2)
```

Implicitly Unwrapped Optionals

Sometimes, there are optional values with a guaranteed value. These optionals (called **implicitly unwrapped optionals**) could be `nil` when they are defined, but, when we access them, we can be certain that their value is non-`nil`. When this is the case, we won't need to unwrap the optional value, as there is a guaranteed value. The optional will "automatically unwrap."

 However, note that if there is a `nil` value when we access the value, the code will fail.

To define an implicitly unwrapped optional, instead of using a question mark at the end of the value type, use an exclamation point. Let's redo our `num1` variable declaration as an implicitly unwrapped optional:

```
1    var num1: Int! = 1
```

Because it is safe to assume that `num1` is not a `nil` value, we can define `num2` and add the two variables together without needing to unwrap `num1`:

```
1    var num1: Int! = 1
2    var num2: Int = 2
3
4    print(num1 + num2) // No unwrapping needed
```

Optional Binding

Recall the earlier example where we defined an optional variable `myString` and written an `if else` statement to check whether it was `nil`. **Optional Binding** is a neat way of simplifying this process of checking whether an optional variable contains a value. It also allows us to extract the value of an optional value, if there is one, into an unwrapped form.

An optional binding in an `if` statement looks as follows:

```
if let constantValue = optionalValue {
        // optionalValue is not nil
        // do something with constantValue
} else {
        // optionalValue is nil
}
```

Let's try it on an example similar to the one earlier:

```
1    var myString: String? = "Hello!"
2
3    if let theString = myString {
4            print(theString)
5    } else {
6            print("myString is nil")
7    }
```

The statement first checks whether myString has a value or not. If it does, it unwraps that value and extracts it into a constant variable called theString. Note that due to the scope of theString, it is only available in the if statement.

After the unwrapped value is extracted, theString can be accessed in the if statement without unwrapping it (as it is already technically an unwrapped value). If myString was originally nil, the theString variable would never be created. The code would execute the else block.

Nil Coalescing and The Ternary Operator

The final concept relating to optionals we will look at is **nil coalescing**, which allows for defining a default value when an optional value is nil.

The nil coalescing operator (??) returns a value is definitely non-nil. The value can either be the value of the optional that it is placed on or the default value that we give it.

Look at the following example to see how it works:

```
1   let myScore: Int? = nil
2
3   let resultScore = myScore ?? 0
4   print(resultScore)
```

After this code is executed, resultScore is set to an unwrapped zero, causing the console to output 0.

The nil coalescing operator can also be used to make printing out optional values easier, so that we don't have to explicitly check for a nil value, but rather have a default in case of nil.

Recall when we had an optionally wrapped myString variable within an if else structure (we have done two examples like this in this chapter, either one works). Now, instead of checking to see whether the value is nil, we can print print(myString ?? "nil value") instead of having to write out a full control flow loop. Simple!

What's actually behind the scenes is a clever shortcut called the ternary conditional (ternary for short) operator.

The **ternary conditional operator** is a special type of operator that evaluates a condition similar to an `if` statement. Imagine the following `if` statement:

```
if condition {
        answer1
} else {
        answer2
}
```

This simple `if` statement can be replaced with a ternary operator that is written in the form `condition ? answer1 : answer2`. It serves as a shortcut for evaluating a single expression given a condition, rather than having to create an `if` loop for a simple task.

For instance, if we wanted to assign a variable called `licenseType` dependent on whether a variable age was at or over 18, we could write the following ternary expression:

```
licenseType = age >= 18 ? "Normal" : "Minor"
```

The nil coalescing expression is an abbreviated ternary operator that has the following equivalence:

```
value != nil ? value! : default
```

The nil coalescing expression evaluates to a ternary operator expression that says that "If `value` is not `nil`, then evaluate to the unwrapped `value`. If `value` is `nil`, evaluate to `default`."

Core OOP Concepts

As with all Object-Oriented programming languages, it is important to understand the fundamental theories and concepts at play within Swift. Throughout this section, we have picked up a number of different techniques and concepts, but haven't tied them to the larger topics that compose all of OOP. Before ending this chapter, let's run through four of the most important concepts in the higher OOP realm. We've already defined and discussed some of the following concepts, but we haven't tagged them with the important keywords that will appear whenever discussing OOP. Let's get to it!

Abstraction

Abstraction is a simple concept that involves the use of classes, functions, objects, and variables. Throughout this book, you've learned about how to create each of the components. Each can be used to represent more complex code in a simple manner. Whenever we initialize a class or call a function, we only access its functionality, while hiding its implementation.

For instance, take the example of a car. When we drive a car, we are only able to access two pedals to change the speed: the accelerator and the brake. Though these two pedals have much more engineering behind them, we don't directly access the functionality of the ignition, cylinders, brake pads, etc. This fundamental, where we show the accessible form of an object, but hide its implementation, is **abstraction**.

Abstraction allows not only for very useful tools, but also for reusability within code. It is the fundamental component of Object-Oriented Programming that allows for programmers to define dynamic structures and objects once and access them without needing to re-implement them each time. When creating classes, we are defining something abstract, as it is not actual physically existent (it's only a "blueprint"). However, the abstraction process allows for multiple objects to be created from the class definition without re-defining code each time.

Encapsulation

Another fundamental concept is encapsulation, which is a specific strategy used as part of abstraction. The two are often confused, but we need to view abstraction as a more general idea and encapsulation as the process that implements that idea. The fundamentals of object and variable scope facilitate encapsulation, which is centered around protecting private attributes and functions of a class while maintaining functionality. Formally, encapsulation is restricting access to certain data structures in groups.

Revisiting the car analogy, encapsulation is the restriction for directly accessing the engine from the driver's seat. There are certain components of the engine that we do not want anyone to meddle with, and therefore, those components are hidden away by a physical barrier to keep the engine from being jeopardized from the outside.

Similarly, instead of using physical barriers, OOP languages like Swift utilize scope to create code barriers between code that implements an object and the private code in the implemented class. This way, internal implementations can be encapsulated in OOP to prevent unrestricted access. More so than scope, however, encapsulation in Swift requires keywords called access modifiers to characterize which attributes of a data structure can be accessed where. There are four main access modifiers in Swift:

- `public`: this access modifier allows the defined variable/attribute/class to be accessible from *any* source file or module/framework that has a path to the item. It has some restrictions on subclassing, whereas the less common `open` modifier does not have these restrictions.
- `internal`: the default access modifier is `internal`, which allows accessibility from *any* source file *inside* the current module/framework.
- `fileprivate`: this one is pretty straightforward, as it only allows access in the *source file* that the item is defined in.
- `private`: only allows for access in the encapsulating block in which the item is defined (similar to how scope works in loops).

We won't be using these access modifiers too much in our apps, but, as you start making advanced apps (or libraries), they will become crucial. For instance, in a banking program, the function to access a bank account will probably be `internal`, so people can view their balance from the interface. However, the actual attributes that store the bank balance will have to be `private` so that nobody can override the values for the balance from outside the class (which is abstracted).

Inheritance

Another key concept we have already discussed in detail is subclassing, which lies under the realm of **inheritance**. Inheritance is the creation and implementation of a new object or class based on the characteristics of another class. The main advantage of inheritance is that programs can build on top of existing code without needing to redefine existing components. The two ways of creating objects that inherit from other ones is by either creating subclasses or extensions. Extensions are similar to subclasses in that they add on to an already existing class but are different because they do not reserve their own identity; they are referenced by the original class name. To review subclasses, go back to Chapter 8 to see subclassing and inheritance in action.

Polymorphism

Polymorphism is a vital part of OOP, describing the capability for objects, classes, and methods to have multiple forms at the same time. It is a requirement for any programming language to be Object-Oriented.

There are a few ways that polymorphism is used in Swift. The first is when creating subclasses of an object. When creating a subclass, say a `Sedan` class from a `Car` superclass, the subclass (`Sedan`) is demonstrating polymorphism, as it is not only a `Sedan`, but is also a `Car`. If there was a part of your code (say a function or other object) that needed a `Car` object, a `Sedan` object could also be passed, as it has the capability to have both forms.

The second way polymorphism works is through **method overloading**, which is having multiple functions with the same function name but different combinations of inputs (we did this with the `init` functions in Chapter 9). There is actually only one method, but it is defined multiple times, with different types of parameters for each definition. Thus, the function exhibits polymorphism by having multiple forms. In addition, functions can exhibit class polymorphism by having parameters or return types of a more generic type. For instance, if we set the parameter for our functions to be the `Car` class, the function would exhibit polymorphism by allowing parameters of `Sedan` type or `Coupe` type.

Chapter Summary

You are doing fantastic! Give yourself a pat on the back, because we just finished learning all the Object-Oriented Programming concepts you'll need to make some powerful apps. Object-Oriented Programming is a huge realm, though, so there is still much more out there to learn and explore. However, we have covered the basics, as well as some more advanced concepts, which will be put to use in our currency-converting app in the next chapter, as well as in the following apps we create. We've completed all of the Playground and theoretical concepts in this book. Now, it's time to put our skills to use.

To recap all that we covered in this chapter:

Variable and Object Scope

- **Lifetime** is the period of time for which a certain item is available within a program's memory
- **Scope** of an item represents the amount of code for which an item is accessible (related but different to lifetime)
- The scope of an item is dependent on where it was initially declared
- Variable scope is limited to the level of code which it is at, including any nested levels
- Global scope represents widely-accessible variables; local scope variables are confined only to a few levels of hierarchy
- **Shadowing** represents the preference of a local variable over a global one if both have the same name
- Frameworks and libraries can be accessed using the `import` keyword

Optional Types

- The `nil` **value** is a valid value for all optional variable types
- Optional types are distinct yet closely related to their non-optional counterparts
- An optional type can be defined the same way as a non-optional, with a `?` appended to it
- Optionals can be **wrapper types**, wrapping values in `Optional()`
- Optional types can be forcibly **unwrapped** by appending an exclamation point (`!`) to the end of the variable
- **Implicitly Unwrapped Optionals** are used when an optional type is guaranteed to not be equal to `nil` at the time of use
- **Optional Binding** is used in conjunction with `if else` structures to check if a value is `nil` and/or extract a non-`nil` value
- **Nil coalescing** allows for evaluating a `nil` value with a default value
- Nil coalescing is a special type of ternary operator
- The **ternary operator** evaluates to one of two values depending on a boolean value (similar to an `if` statement)

Core OOP Concepts

- **Abstraction** allows for creating abstract classes which can be reused and accessed multiple times in the form of an object
- **Encapsulation** restricts access to certain data structures without hindering the implementation of an object
- **Inheritance** allows for reusing certain components of a class in a new class without recreating an entirely new set of code
- **Polymorphism** is the capability for objects and methods to exhibit multiple forms at one time

End-of-Chapter Exercises

1) Lifetime and scope are two different concepts.

(A) True

(B) False

2) Which of the following will throw a scope error?

```
(A) let itemA = "A"
    func functionName() {
        let itemB = "B"
        item = itemB + itemA
    }
```

```
(B) let itemA = "A"
    let itemB = "B"
    func functionName() {
        item = itemB + itemA
    }
    item = itemB + itemA
```

```
(C) func functionName() {
        let itemA = "A"
        let itemB = "B"
        item = itemB + itemA
    }
```

```
(D) func functionName() {
        let itemA = "A"
        let itemB = "B"
    }
    item = itemB + itemA
```

3) Given the following function, what will be the output if `show(value: 5)` is run?

```
value = 3

func show(value: Int) {
        print(value)
}
```

(A) 5

(B) 3

(C) None of the above

4) `String` and `String?` are the same type and can be used interchangeably:

(A) True

(B) False

5) `myNum: Int? = nil` is a valid statement:

(A) True

(B) False

6) `myNum: Int = nil` is a valid statement:

(A) True

(B) False

7) What will the output of the following statement be?

```
myName: String? = "Etash"
print(myName)
```

(A) `"Etash"`

(B) `Etash`

(C) `Optional("Etash")`

(D) The `print` statement will throw an error.

8) Given the following line of code:

```
let num1: Int? = 1
let num2: Int? = 2
```

Which of the following will not throw an error?

(A) num1 + num2

(B) num1! + num2

(C) num1 + num2!

(D) num1! + num2!

9) Given the following declaration:

```
var number: Int! = 10
```

Which of the following will throw an error?

(A) number = nil

(B) number = 5

(C) number = 5?

(D) None of the above

10) After the following code is executed:

```
var myScore: Int? = nil
var resultScore = myScore ?? 0
```

What are the values of myScore and resultScore?

(A) 0,0

(B) nil,nil

(C) nil,0

(D) 0,nil

11) After the following code is executed:

```
let id = 234567
let type = id > 200000 ? "Student" : "Teacher"
```

What is the value of `type`?

(A) 234567

(B) "Student"

(C) "Teacher"

(D) The ternary conditional operator is incorrect.

12) Which of the following is the capability for objects and methods to exhibit multiple forms at one time?

(A) Abstraction

(B) Encapsulation

(C) Inheritance

(D) Polymorphism

13) Which of the following allows for creating classes that can be reused and accessed multiple times in the form an object?

(A) Abstraction

(B) Encapsulation

(C) Inheritance

(D) Polymorphism

14) Which of the following allows for reusing certain components of a class in a new class without recreating an entirely new set of code?

(A) Abstraction

(B) Encapsulation

(C) Inheritance

(D) Polymorphism

15) Which of the following restricts access to certain data structures without hindering the implementation of an object?

(A) Abstraction

(B) Encapsulation

(C) Inheritance

(D) Polymorphism

Answers

1. A
2. D
3. A
4. B
5. A
6. B
7. C
8. D
9. C
10. C
11. B
12. D
13. A
14. C
15. B

Answer Explanations

1) **(A)** The scope of the item represents the section of code for which an item is accessible, whereas the lifetime of an item is the period of time for which an item is available in memory.

2) **(D)** In option D, `itemA` and `itemB` are defined in a lower level of scope than the line in which they are accesssed, thus they cannot be accessed.

3) **(A)** When the function is run, the parameter `value` becomes 5. When `print(value)` is called, the closest level of scope is this parameter. Thus, 5 is printed, as the parameter `value` shadows the `value` variable outside of the function.

4) **(B)** Optionals and non-optionals cannot be used interchangeably.

5) **(A)** `myNum` can be `nil` since it is defined as an optional `Int?`

6) **(B)** `myNum` cannot be `nil` since it is defined as a non-optional `Int`

7) **(C)** Since the value of `myName` is optional and unwrapped when it is printed, the value printed will be `Optional("Etash")`

8) **(D)** For optional values to be added or operated, they must be unwrapped. The only option in which both optionals are unwrapped is D.

9) **(C)** Raw integers with an optional chain (?) are invalid in Swift.

10) **(C)** The value of `myScore` was unchanged; it is `nil`. Since `myScore` is `nil`, the `nil` coalescer for `resultScore` evaluates to the default value, which is 0.

11) **(B)** Since `id` is greater than `200000`, the boolean expression `id > 200000` evaluates to true. Thus, the ternary operator returns the first expression, which is `"Student."`

12) **(D)** See chapter conclusion.

13) **(A)** See chapter conclusion.

14) **(C)** See chapter conclusion.

15) **(B)** See chapter conclusion.

Chapter Eleven: Using OOP In Your Apps (App #3)

Introduction

In the past several chapters, we gathered a huge toolset of advanced programming concepts and skills to apply in our apps. Through learning Object-Oriented Programming skills, we can create and use classes, functions, optionals, and more.

In this chapter, we will put some of these skill sets to use by developing a "Currency Conversion" app, which will be able to convert certain amounts of money from one currency to another. The app will use a few OOP concepts, mostly functions, to show how we can start to use some dynamics within our apps. The app will also apply the items we learned in the previous section of the book, such as program flow, data structures, and optionals.

"Currency Converter" App

The user flow of the app we're creating is fairly simple. The user will be able to convert money from one of four different currencies into another currency. The amount of money will be inputted using a text field, and the currencies will be selected using an option picker.

To facilitate the conversion process, we'll create a `Currency` class to hold the value and country of a certain amount of money. We will also write a custom function, which takes in the currency amount a Currency object holds and converts it to or from a certain currency depending on the parameters. We will also have a dictionary to store the conversion amounts.

Designing the App

First, as always, we will create the layout of the app. Create a new Xcode project titled "Currency Converter" and select Single View Application.

Adding Label, Text Field, and Constraints

After starting up a new project, go to the `Main.Storyboard` file to set up the text fields and option selectors for the conversion process. First, add a label and a text field at the top of the page and stretch them horizontally (*Figure 11-1*).

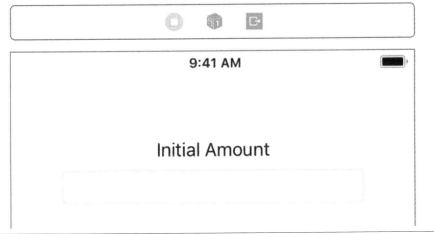

Figure 11-1

Now, add constraints for the two items. Add the following constraints on the label first (*Figure 11-2*):

- Height of 25 Points
- 50 Points below top of view
- 50 Points from left of view
- 50 Points from right of view

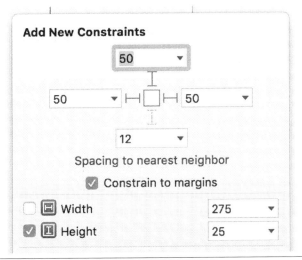

Figure 11-2

The label is now anchored vertically from the top, with a vertical height limit, and anchored horizontally from the left and the right.

Next, add the following constraints for the text field (*Figure 11-3*):

- Height of 30 Points
- 20 Points below nearest neighbor (label)
- 50 Points from left of view
- 50 Points from right of view

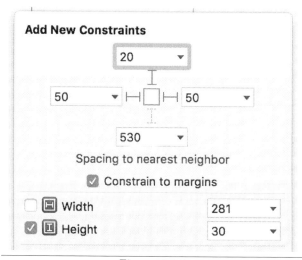

Figure 11-3

 Additionally, select **Decimal Pad** as the Keyboard Type in the attributes for the text field. The option can be accessed in the right utility pane of the storyboard after selecting the text field.

Adding Currency Pickers

Let's add the two currency pickers, which will represent the initial currency and the final currency of the conversion. We will use the UISegmentedControl (found on the utility pane of the storyboard) to allow users to pick from one of several options (*Figure 11-4*).

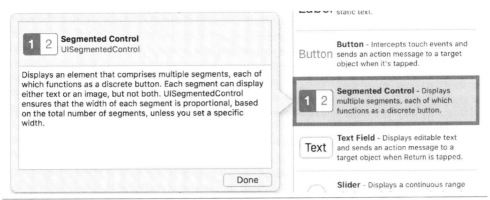

Figure 11-4

Before adding the first of the two segmented controls, let's add a label to indicate to the user that the first segmented control is the starting currency.

This label, `"Initial Currency Type,"` can be placed underneath the text field, with the following constraints:

- Height of 25 Points
- 50 Points below nearest neighbor (text field)
- 50 Points from left of view
- 50 Points from right of view

These constraints are the same as those shown for the first label in *Figure 11-2*.

After adding the label, drag a `UISegmentedControl` from the right utility pane into the view controller on the storyboard, placing it beneath the newly created label. After doing so, change the number of segments in the object to 4, by selecting the object in our view and changing the `Segments` property at the top of the utility pane (*Figure 11-5*).

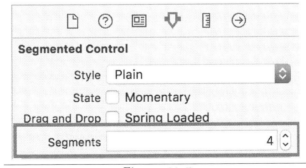

Figure 11-5

Add 20-50-50-30 Constraints to the Segmented Control, representing 20 points from top neighbor, 50 points from left, 50 points from right, and 30 points for the height of the segmented control (same relative constraints as the text field in *Figure 11-3*).

After adding constraints and ensuring the control object has 4 segments, rename the segment groups to Dollar, Yen, Euro, and Pound.

This can be done by double clicking on each segment to open a text field where the name of the segment can be inputted or using the top of the utility panel to select each segment (*Figure 11-6*) and changing its Title attribute.

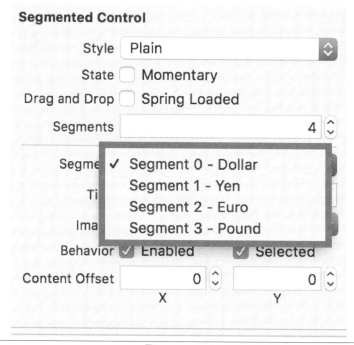

Figure 11-6

After this, add the label and the segmented control for the final currency type. Recreate the same label and segmented control we created for the initial currency type and place them below the existing components on the view controller.

The label should have (50-50-50-25) constraints for (top, left, right, height) and the segmented control should have (20-50-50-30) constraints after being placed beneath its respective label. Thus, the view controller should look similar to *Figure 11-7* (before adding final components).

Final Layout

Lastly, our application will require two more things: a button and another label. Upon button press, the inputted initial amount from the initial currency should be converted to the final currency and the final amount should be displayed with a label.

Add a button titled "Convert" and a label with a default number (say 00.00) underneath the existing components. The text of the label does not matter as we will programmatically change it after converting the currency. Be sure to add constraints similar to the previous items! After adding all our components, the final application layout should look like the following:

9:41 AM

Initial Amount

Initial Currency Type

| Dollar | Yen | Euro | Pound |

Final Currency Type

| Dollar | Yen | Euro | Pound |

Convert

0.00

Figure 11-7

If you're up for it, use the right utility panel to customize the component colors and fonts to add some user interface (UI) design!

Connecting and Understanding Layout Components

Now, let's transition to coding the app. First, connect each of the Main.Storyboard components to the counterpart ViewController.swift file, as you have done in previous apps. Open up the dual (assistant) editor mode from the top-right toolbar in Xcode.

Next, code reference the two UISegmentedControls we created in our layout. Remember objects can be referenced from the Main.Storyboard file by pressing the control key and dragging from the reference object to the line of code where we want the object to exist. After referencing the segmented controls as "initialCurrency" and "finalCurrency" in the viewController class (but not inside a function), your code should look as follows:

```
11   class ViewController: UIViewController {
12          @IBOutlet weak var finalCurrency: UISegmentedControl!
13          @IBOutlet weak var initialCurrency: UISegmentedControl!
14          ...
15   }
```

Notice how we placed these two code references *in* the class viewController. This allows the scope to be limited so that only code blocks in viewController can directly access these objects. They are also placed *outside* of the class functions such as viewDidLoad() to allow those objects to be accessible in any function. If they were placed inside a function, only that function would directly be able to access them.

In addition, referencing @IBOutlet objects is a perfect example of OOP in action. Though we are not defining a class in these statements, the var keyword shows these two lines are similar to defining a variable, which holds an object. The two preceding words, weak and @IBOutlet, are modifiers that change the way the variable functions. The two objects are both a part of the UISegmentedControl class, which is already defined in the Swift language. All we did was create instances of these classes on the Main.Storyboard file and reference those objects through these variables (there's much more going on behind the scenes). Recall objects are passed by reference. Therefore, when we reference these objects to the variables in our code, they do not duplicate the UISegementedControl but rather reference to the exact instance that we created on the layout page. Pretty cool!

Notice the exclamation point at the end of UISegmentedControl in the referencing variable. It indicates an optional! More specifically, if you remember from the previous chapter, this exclamation point represents an implicitly unwrapped optional. Therefore, whenever our code tries to access it, the compiler will guarantee that this object exists. We know that there are physical objects created on our storyboard that are referenced by that variable. If we were to delete those objects, however, our code would crash, as the compiler would guarantee that there is a non-nil object where, in fact, it does not exist. This helps maintain order in our code and ensure that there is a guaranteed object on the storyboard for every object we reference.

After referencing the two segmented controls, do the same for the text field and the final result label.

Since we only need to access the attributes, such as the text or selected segment, of these objects (segmented controls, text fields, labels), create their references as "Outlet" objects, as so:

```
12      @IBOutlet weak var finalCurrency: UISegmentedControl!
13
14      @IBOutlet weak var initialCurrency: UISegmentedControl!
15
16      @IBOutlet weak var initialAmountTextField: UITextField!
17
18      @IBOutlet weak var finalAmountLabel: UILabel!
```

The button, on the other hand, does not need to be referenced as just an object. We don't need to access any *attributes* of the button, but rather need the button to trigger a *function*. The function reference type, as we briefly discussed when creating our first two apps, is an **Action** reference.

Reference the "Convert" button as an Action function below (outside) the viewDidLoad() function. Action can be selected under the "Connection" type after control+dragging from the button to the code. Call this function buttonClicked and leave all other reference options alone; they simply indicate ways the button can be tapped—we'll use the default button tap options.

As you can see, instead of creating a variable that references an object, the Action type creates a function (keyword func) called buttonClicked with a parameter called sender which has type Any.

```
25      @IBAction func buttonClicked(_ sender: Any) {
26          }
```

 The type Any is a superclass of all objects in Swift. Using the principle of polymorphism, all Swift objects are inherently subclasses of Any. Therefore, they take both the form of the object type they are defined to be and the form of Any. This allows functions like buttonClicked to take "any" type of object in as a parameter. Polymorphism, in this case, allows for the same function to be applied to buttons, labels, text fields, or any other type of object without creating unique functions for every available object.

Instead of manually calling the buttonClicked() function, whenever a user presses the connected button, the button will call the function and pass its own reference key as the sender: Any object. This way, we can perform the conversion between currencies in the function whenever someone presses the button. Additionally, if we wanted to change any attributes of the button from which buttonClicked() was called, we could through sender, which references the button on the app layout.

Accessing Input Values

Everything from the Main.Storyboard layout is now connected to the ViewController.swift file. All we need to do is code procedures to extract the initial value, initial currency type, and final currency type and use that information to yield a final value, which we'll plug into the finalAmountLabel.

First, we will use the button function to extract the needed values for currency conversion. To do so, create three variables to store the initial value and each of the two selected segments. At this time, you can revert back to the single standard editor.

Retrieving and Casting the Initial Value

First, create a let variable (permanent variable) called initialAmount and set its value to initialAmountTextField.text, where we retrieve the text attribute of our text field object. Notice we created a permanent variable instead of a normal dynamic one. Because we do not need to or want to change the user's number, we use let to ensure the value never changes.

```
25   @IBAction func buttonClicked(_ sender: Any) {
26           let initialAmount = initialAmountTextField.text
27   }
```

Notice text is actually an optional String type:

The text displayed by the text field.

String? text

Figure 11-8

This is an issue, because we want initialAmount to be a Float variable, so that its value can be multiplied by a ratio and converted it. A String type does not allow for this.

Thus, we can attempt to cast this variable by enclosing the attribute statement in a Float() cast:

```
26           let initialAmount = Float(initialAmountTextField.text)
```

There's another problem! The text attribute is an optional variable as well, so when we use the Float() cast to convert it from String? to Float, there's an error. The compiler can't determine whether the text field is empty (text is nil), so it throws an error when trying to cast an optional type, since casting non-existent nil values can crash the application.

Therefore, we have a few different options to ensure the optional attribute is not nil and convert the non-nil value to a non-optional type. The easiest solution is to force unwrap the attribute from the text field using the ! unwrapper. Though this will remove the compiler error, only force unwrapping the attribute can throw a runtime error.

 Think about why force unwrapping the optional `text` attribute from our `initialAmountTextField` might throw a runtime error...what might we do to fix the issue?

The issue with force unwrapping `initialAmountTextField.text!` is that forced unwrapping requires the value is non-`nil` at the time of unwrapping. However, the `text` attribute can still be `nil` (or not). We can't know for sure until the user uses the app. Therefore, if the text field was left blank and we tried to force unwrap the empty value, we would encounter a runtime error and our app could crash. Therefore, to force unwrap, we first have to guarantee the value is not `nil`.

The first way of doing so is using an `if` statement. We can check if the `text` attribute is `nil` and set the `initialAmount` variable equal to 0 if it is (we will treat a blank amount as a zero amount). Because the `initialAmount` value needs to be accessed outside of the `if` statement, it will have to be defined as a mutable (`var`) variable before the `if` block with a generic `Float()` value and then referenced within the block. In the `else` block, where it's guaranteed to not be `nil`, we can force unwrap the `text` value and cast it using `Float()`.

```
26      var initialAmount = Float()
27      if initialAmountTextField.text == nil {
28              initialAmount = 0
29      } else {
30              initialAmount = Int(initialAmountTextField.text!)!
31      }
```

Don't write this code yet, though! There's an **even easier** way to do this—with less work, fewer lines of code, and more clarity. Remember nil coalescing? We set `initialAmount` equal to a default value (0) if the text field is blank and equal to the unwrapped value of the text field otherwise. This is exactly what the nil coalescing sequence does in one elegant line of code, instead of six.

```
1   let initialAmount = Float(initialAmount.text ?? "0")
```

 Notice we put `"0"`, not 0, at the end of the first part of the nil coalescer. There are two reasons for using a `String`. First, we are already casting the value inside the parentheses (the value that is evaluated by the nil coalescer) to a `Float`. Therefore, it is fine to have a `String` value inside the parentheses. Secondly, a nil coalescer must evaluate to a consistent type, whether the placed value is `nil` or not. Therefore, since the unwrapped version of `initialAmountTextField.text` is a `String`, our default value must also be a `String`.

After this first part, we need the compiler to confirm that even if this statement resolves to a failed cast (which could happen if the `String` value is not `nil` but also not convertible), there is a backup default value. Failed casts can result in `nil` if the `String` is unconvertible, so we will add a second nil coalescer. The code inside the button function should be one line:

```
25  @IBAction func buttonClicked(_ sender: Any) {
26          let initialAmount = Float(initialAmountTextField.text ?? "0") ?? 0
27  }
```

Retrieving Selected Segment Values

Perfect! Now it's time to move onto getting the selected values of initial and final currency from our segmented controls. The `UISegmentedControl` property that represents the selected tab is the `selectedSegmentIndex` attribute. Instead of being an attribute that accesses the String `title` (text) of the selected segment, the `selectedSegmentIndex` is an Integer. Similar to an array index key, this index represents the number of the segment which is selected in our segmented control, starting from 0 at the left-most segment. Based on *Figure 11-6*, the 0 index represents "Dollar," 1 represents "Yen," 2 represents "Euro," and 3 represents "Pound."

Create two constant variables, `initialCurrencyIndex` and `finalCurrencyIndex`, and set them equal to their respective segment indices. Since `UISegmentedControl` will **always** have a selected value, the `selectedSegmentIndex` attribute is a non-optional `Int`, so there is no need to unwrap it:

```
27          let initialCurrencyIndex = initialCurrency.selectedSegmentIndex
28          let finalCurrencyIndex = finalCurrency.selectedSegmentIndex
```

We could convert these indices into the respective `String` currencies they represent, but we will send the indices to a conversion function (one that we create ourself) in a moment.

Now, all of the input components from the `Main.Storyboard` file have been accounted for. Let's continue and create the conversion function.

Creating the Conversion Function

The conversion function requires three input parameters: the initial amount (`initialAmount`), the initial currency type (`initialCurrencyIndex`), and the final currency type (`finalCurrencyIndex`). The function will return a `Float` as the final converted answer.

Let's start by defining the header line of the conversion function, `convert()`, underneath the button function.

```
func convert(initialAmount: Float, initialCurrencyIndex: Int, finalCurrencyIndex: Int) -> Float {
}                                            ⓘ Missing return in a function expected to return 'Float'
```

Figure 11-9

Notice that there is an error when we initially define this function. Since the function is empty, it does not return the `Float` value that it promises to return. Ignore the error for now—it will disappear after we finish the function.

On the first line, define an array with conversion factors for each currency.

```
33        let factors = [1, 112, 0.86, 0.77] as [Float]
```

This list shows the equivalent amount of each currency for one dollar. Thus, one dollar is one dollar, 112 yen, 0.86 euro, and 0.77 pounds. These values will be used as conversion factors by dividing the initial value by the initial factor and multiplying it by the final factor to yield the final value (math not shown). This method makes it easier to have a common standard factor between all the currencies, instead of having 12 different numbers to represent "euro to yen," "yen to euro," "pound to dollar," etc. Notice we set the array so that it has the same indices as the currency's respective segment.

We also cast the array to make sure it is composed of `Float` types, rather than `Double`. At this level, it doesn't matter if we use `Double` or `Float` since they are both decimal point types that can store the values for our purpose. However, the function parameters are `Float`, the conversion factors must also be of `Float` type if they are to be used in calculations.

After defining the array, create two variables, `initialFactor` and `finalFactor`, that retrieve the factor of the respective currencies using `initialCurrencyIndex` and `finalCurrencyIndex`.

```
35        let initialFactor = factors[initialCurrencyIndex]
36        let finalFactor = factors[finalCurrencyIndex]
```

All of the values needed to determine the final value have been defined now. Create a final variable called `finalAmount` and set it equal to `initialAmount` divided by `initialFactor` and multiplied by `finalFactor`:

```
38        let finalAmount = initialAmount / initialFactor * finalFactor
```

We divide the initial amount in one currency by its conversion factor to yield a common number of units. The common number of units (which is actually just number of dollars) is multiplied by a second conversion factor to yield the final amount in units of the final currency.

But wait! There's just one more line of code we need. Remember we were getting an error because we didn't return a value? To solve this issue, `return finalAmount`. The `convert()` function is complete.

```
32   func convert(initialAmount: Float, initialCurrencyIndex: Int, finalCurrencyIndex: In\
33   t) -> Float {
34           let factors = [1, 112, 0.86, 0.77] as [Float]
35
36           let initialFactor = factors[initialCurrencyIndex]
37           let finalFactor = factors[finalCurrencyIndex]
38
39           let finalAmount = initialAmount / initialFactor * finalFactor
40
41           return finalAmount
42   }
```

Final Steps

After creating the conversion function, we need to pass the values we extracted in the button function to the conversion function, and retrieve the finalAmount that the conversion function outputs. First, let's call the function. Type 'convert(' in the buttonClicked() function to see Xcode auto-fill the parameters of the convert() function (*Figure 11-10*).

```
convert(
    Float (initialAmount: Float, initialCurrencyIndex: Int, finalCurrencyIndex: Int)
```

Figure 11-10

Use these parameters by pressing enter. Then, for each parameter, plug in the respective local variables extracted in the button function:

```
30   convert(initialAmount: initialAmount,
31           initialCurrencyIndex: initialCurrencyIndex,
32           finalCurrencyIndex: finalCurrencyIndex)
```

This statement passes each parameter to the convert() function, executes the function, and evaluates to the return value of the function. To store the finalAmount the function returns, create a variable and set it equal to the function call:

```
30   let finalAmount = convert(initialAmount: initialAmount,
31           initialCurrencyIndex: initialCurrencyIndex,
32           finalCurrencyIndex: finalCurrencyIndex)
```

Notice that, in the function call, each of the local variables in the buttonClicked() function is a distinct variable from the convert() function parameters, which have the same name. These two sets of variables have separate scopes limited to their functions and cannot be accessed between functions. When the parameters are passed to the convert() function call, the values of the variables are being passed, not the actual variable. See *Figure 11-11*, which illustrates the path that each of the variables and parameters take from the buttonClicked() function to the convert() function.

```
     @IBAction func buttonClicked(_ sender: Any) {
26       let initialAmount = Float(initialAmountTextField.text ?? "0") ?? 0
27       let initialCurrencyIndex = initialCurrency.selectedSegmentIndex
28       let finalCurrencyIndex = finalCurrency.selectedSegmentIndex
29
30       let finalAmount = convert(initialAmount: initialAmount, initialCurrencyIndex:
            initialCurrencyIndex, finalCurrencyIndex: finalCurrencyIndex)
31   }
32
33   func convert(initialAmount: Float, initialCurrencyIndex: Int, finalCurrencyIndex: Int) -> Float {
34       let factors = [1, 112, 0.86, 0.77] as [Float]
35
36       let initialFactor = factors[initialCurrencyIndex]
37       let finalFactor = factors[finalCurrencyIndex]
38
39       let finalAmount = initialAmount / initialFactor * finalFactor
40
41       return finalAmount
42   }
```

Figure 11-11

The red represents the local variables for the buttonClicked() function, the blue represents the passed parameter values for the convert() function, and the pink represents the reference to the parameter variable in the convert() function. Thus, the finalCurrencyIndex in the buttonClicked() function is distinct from the finalCurrencyIndex in the convert() function (and likewise for the three parameters).

The last thing to be done is set the text of the finalAmountLabel equal to the finalAmount. Since finalAmount is a Float type and text must be a String, cast the finalAmount as a String type:

```
32   finalAmountLabel.text = String(finalAmount)
```

We have everything set up! There is one final step that will ensure our User Interface (UI) works seamlessly.

Remember that we have a text field in our app. This text field, when activated, will trigger the testing device to show a keyboard, which may cover some of the components in our app. Making the keyboard hide when the user taps outside of the keyboard area will require a few more lines of code.

First, in the class definition for ViewController, set the class type to act as both a UIViewController class and a UITextFieldDelegate class by adding a comma after UIViewController and typing UITextFieldDelegate:

```
11   class ViewController: UIViewController, UITextFieldDelegate {
12   ...
13   }
```

After doing this, we need to confirm the delegate for initialAmountTextField is equal to the ViewController class, which can be referenced using the self keyword. In the viewDidLoad()

function, which is called whenever the `ViewController` is initialized, set the `.delegate` attribute equal to `self` (Line 22):

```
20  override func viewDidLoad() {
21          super.viewDidLoad()
22          initialAmountTextField.delegate = self
23  }
```

This ensures our `ViewController` has the proper functions to control the behavior of the text field. Though the `viewDidLoad()` function is not an initializer function, it acts similarly to one, which is why we put any "setup" tasks, such as delegation, in this function.

Lastly, after the `ViewController` class is delegated to control the `initialAmountTextField`, write a new function (starting with `override func`) called `touchesBegan`. If Swift does not auto-fill the `touchesBegan` function, type the following code in the `ViewController` class:

```
27  override func touchesBegan(_ touches: Set<UITouch>, with event: UIEvent?) {
28  }
```

The `touchesBegan` function is triggered whenever a user touches outside of the keyboard area. When this happens, we want the `ViewController` delegate to end the keyboard, which can be done by calling the `endEditing()` function:

```
27  override func touchesBegan(_ touches: Set<UITouch>, with event: UIEvent?) {
28          self.view.endEditing(true)
29  }
```

Congratulations! You have completed the app and can now test it on an Xcode device (or your own if you connect it to Xcode). Select a testing device in the Xcode toolbar and press run. After launching, you'll see that the app is fully functioning and can use the text field and segmented controls to convert currencies.

Figure 11-12

Chapter Summary

Again, great job on making your way through this section of the book! You've encountered most of the Object-Oriented concepts needed to make scalable apps and applied those concepts to create a fully-functional application from scratch. In this app, we applied several Object-Oriented and Swift Concepts, including:

- Casting and Types
- Creating Functions
- Passing Parameters and Return Types
- Class Inheritance
- Optional Variables
- Nil Coalescing
- and many more!

You now are well-equipped to start making your own apps using Xcode and Swift. The final two sections of this book will be dedicated to learning more advanced technologies offered by Xcode, but you've already mastered the essential concepts. Each chapter from now on will involve using a new technology to create an app. Get ready for even more functional apps! See you in the next section.

Project Source Code

ViewController.swift

```swift
 9   import UIKit
10
11   class ViewController: UIViewController, UITextFieldDelegate {
12       @IBOutlet weak var finalCurrency: UISegmentedControl!
13
14       @IBOutlet weak var initialCurrency: UISegmentedControl!
15
16       @IBOutlet weak var initialAmountTextField: UITextField!
17
18       @IBOutlet weak var finalAmountLabel: UILabel!
19
20       override func viewDidLoad() {
21           super.viewDidLoad()
22           // Do any additional setup after loading the view, typically from a nib.
23
24           initialAmountTextField.delegate = self
25       }
26
27       override func touchesBegan(_ touches: Set<UITouch>, with event: UIEvent?) {
28           self.view.endEditing(true)
29       }
30
31       @IBAction func buttonClicked(_ sender: Any) {
32           let initialAmount = Float(initialAmountTextField.text ?? "0") ?? 0
33           let initialCurrencyIndex = initialCurrency.selectedSegmentIndex
34           let finalCurrencyIndex = finalCurrency.selectedSegmentIndex
35
36           let finalAmount = convert(initialAmount: initialAmount, initialCurrencyIndex\
37   : initialCurrencyIndex, finalCurrencyIndex: finalCurrencyIndex)
38
39           finalAmountLabel.text = String(finalAmount)
40       }
41
42       func convert(initialAmount: Float, initialCurrencyIndex: Int, finalCurrencyIndex\
43   : Int) -> Float {
44           let factors = [1, 112, 0.86, 0.77] as [Float]
45
46           let initialFactor = factors[initialCurrencyIndex]
```

```
47          let finalFactor = factors[finalCurrencyIndex]
48
49          let finalAmount = initialAmount / initialFactor * finalFactor
50
51          return finalAmount
52      }
53
54      override func didReceiveMemoryWarning() {
55          super.didReceiveMemoryWarning()
56          // Dispose of any resources that can be recreated.
57      }
58
59
60  }
```

Section D: Advanced Features in Swift

In This Section

Chapter Twelve: Table Views and Storage (App #4)

Introduction

Welcome to the fourth section of the book, where we will explore many more features in the Swift language and Development Kit. The section will focus on creating three more apps using new technologies. The first of these apps is a "to-do list," which utilizes several Swift features, such as UITableView, and some permanent storage techniques. The focus of the next three chapters will be to apply fundamentals from Sections A, B, and C, and learn to integrate more advanced features in your apps. Let's get started!

To-Do List: App Overview

This app will allow users to do three things: add to-do items to a list of tasks, view all of the list items in a collective space, and tap on list items to view more details about them. The main screen of the application will be the page in which the list items will be listed, using a Swift layout class called UITableView. Table Views display a collection of vertically stacked cells or tabs, each of which contain distinct text.

Each cell in our table view will display the name of a to-do list item. As an item is pressed, the app will transition to a second screen (UIViewController) containing details of the to-do item. Finally, on the main page, which contains the table view, users can press a button to add a new to-do item, which will transition to another UIViewController to put in the details for the to-do item.

Layout Design

Start up a new Xcode project called To-Do List as a Single View Application. In our app, we will need to use a TableViewController rather than the default ViewController, so delete the ViewController.swift file. Additionally, on the storyboard, select the header bar for the View Controller and press delete to remove it from the application.

Navigation and Root View Controllers

On the Main.Storyboard file, from the utility pane on the right, drag out a "Navigation Controller" item. Notice that instead of being one View Controller, the Navigation Controller is a pair of two view controllers linked together by a "segue" (See *Figure 12-1*). The first of the two is a `UINavigationController`, which controls navigation between its "Root View Controller" and other view controllers. The view controller on the right is the "Root View Controller." The Root Controller is of type `UITableViewController`, which can be seen by selecting the identity inspector tab (third icon) on the utility pane. On the attributes inspector of the navigation controller, check the option for "is initial view controller," since the default initial view controller was deleted. This way, the app knows what to display first.

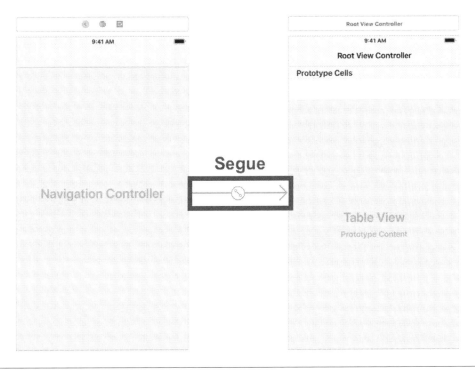

Figure 12-1

Segues are paths that link two view controllers together. Segues trigger the application to transition from one view controller to another, either programmatically or through explicitly defined segues on the `Main.Storyboard`.

Inside the `UITableViewController` on the storyboard, notice the small header at the top of the table view called "Prototype Cells." Underneath this header is a small white space, which can be selected and edited. As the header dictates, the space is a prototype cell for our table view. The prototypes we create on the table view storyboard can be reused and edited programmatically to create custom table views.

In our to-do list, each list tab should have the name of the to-do item and the date by which it needs to be completed. Currently, the default prototype cell for the table view controller supports only one label of text, but we can create a custom cell or use one of the default options to allow for two. Select the white, blank prototype cell that is listed underneath the "prototype cells" header. Inside the utility pane attribute inspector, change the "Style" attribute of the prototype cell from "Custom" to "Subtitle." Upon doing this, two labels will appear on the prototype cell, one with larger text on top and another one with smaller text beneath it. As new to-do list items are created in the app, the table view will create more instances of the prototype cell, setting the "Title" label text to be the name of the item and the "Subtitle" label text to be the date by which it should be completed.

In addition to the four default options for a prototype cell in a table view (Basic, Left Detail, Right Detail, Subtitle), we can also create our own custom prototype cells, which can contain text fields, images, buttons, switches, and other items. These items will then have to set constraints and be connected to a new `UITableViewCell` class. Since these advanced features are outside of the scope of this application, we won't create any custom cells, but know that the capability exists while developing your own apps.

In addition to viewing to-do list items in the table view, users must also be able to add new list items to the app. To facilitate this, add a "Bar Button Item" (**not a normal button**) to the header bar of the Root View (Table View) Controller.

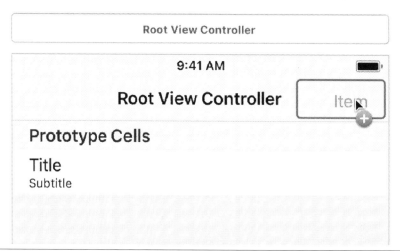

Figure 12-2

 Why not add a button to this header bar?
Theoretically, we could add a normal button item to the header bar of the Root View Controller. However, the Navigation Controller creates a parent header bar (called a navigation bar) for its Root View Controller and any other view controllers that segue off of it. Within the navigation bar, the navigation controller may dynamically change the left and right bar items. Though putting a regular `UIButton` in the navigation bar would likely not affect the way in which the navigation controller controls the bar, `UIBarButtonItems` style better and work more effectively within navigation bars. They also do not require constraints (usually) when paired with other bar items.

Selecting the item and using the utility pane, change the System Item attribute for this button to be "Add," which will change the button from a text button to an add icon.

New Item View Controller

When a user presses this button, a new view controller should appear with options for adding a new to-do list item. To do this, add a new View Controller to the storyboard. To connect the View Controller to the add button, we will use a transition segue. Selecting the add button, hold down the `control` key and drag (the same way as connecting storyboard items to a Swift file) towards the new View Controller (*Figure 12-3*).

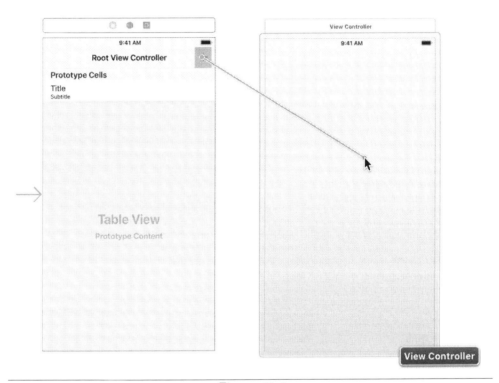

Figure 12-3

Doing so will yield a range of options for adding a segue from the bar button that leads to the view controller. Though all of the options are widely used, the two of most interest to us are the "Show" Segue and the "Present Modally" Segue. The "Show" segue will present the new View Controller as if it were a part of the navigation controller, adding a navigation bar to the top of it. The "Present Modally" segue will show the view controller on top of the rest of the navigational views without it being tied to the navigation controller. Thus, "Present Modally" segue will display the view controller without having a navigation bar connected to the root view controller.

In this app, it won't matter which of the two segues we use for the view controller which adds to-do list items. For the view controllers which display the item details, we need to use the "Show" Segue, though, as the details view controller needs a dynamic "back" button that takes the user back to the root view controller.

Since the app will already demonstrate a "Show" Segue with the list detail views, let's utilize the "Present Modally" Segue for adding list items. Upon performing the `control`+drag from the root view controller, select the "Present Modally" Segue option.

The two View Controllers should now appear to be connected with a segue between them.

Continue setting up with the following steps:

1) On the new controller, drag a "Navigation Bar" to the top of the screen and align it under the app status bar.

2) Then, using the constraints, add:

- a top constraint of 0
- a left constraint of 0
- a right constraint of 0
- a height constraint of 44

This assures that the navigation bar is pushed upwards and horizontally on the view.

3) On the bar, change the title to "Add a New Item" by pressing twice on the navigation bar we just added and changing the attributes using the utility pane. The first click will select the bar itself, and the second click will select the label item that is the bar's title.

4) Add two bar button items to the navigation bar—one on the left and another on the right.

5) Using the attributes inspector, change the bar buttons' System Item attributes so that the left bar button displays "Cancel" and the right button displays "Done." Also, change the Style attribute of the right button to "Done," which bolds the button for stylistic reasons. Both these buttons will need programmatic commands attached to them before segueing back to the main root controller, so do not add segues to either of them.

6) Add two text fields, a text view, and three labels to the view controller. Arrange and retitle them so they look similar to the layout in *Figure 12-4*. Feel free to customize some of the design attributes.

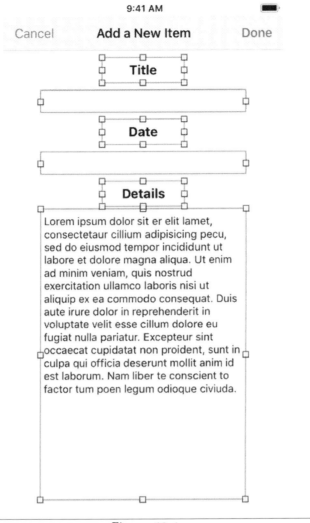

Figure 12-4

7) To secure the constraints of each of these components, add width and height constraints to each of the three labels.

8) Using the alignment constraints, ensure each of the labels is centered horizontally on the screen. Remember that alignment constraints are found in a different tab than the one for the constraints in Step 7.

9) Add a top constraint to the uppermost label to secure it vertically with respect to the navigation bar. Do the same with the text field underneath it, securing it horizontally as well to the sides of the view controller. Repeat this step for all components on the screen.

10) Add a bottom constraint to the text view to secure it to the bottom of the screen (the text view will stretch its height to dynamically fit its top and bottom constraints).

Item Details View Controller

After finishing the view controller to add new items, we need to add another view controller to the storyboard to view the details of each item. The item detail view controller will be very similar to the new item view controller, except it will have non-editable labels and text views instead of editable ones.

We also need a show segue from the root view controller to the item detail view controller. However, since the table view cells are dynamic and can change depending on what the user adds, we must add an unspecified segue from the root view controller to the item detail view. Instead of control+dragging from a button or a table view cell, add a segue from the root view controller header to the respective view controller.

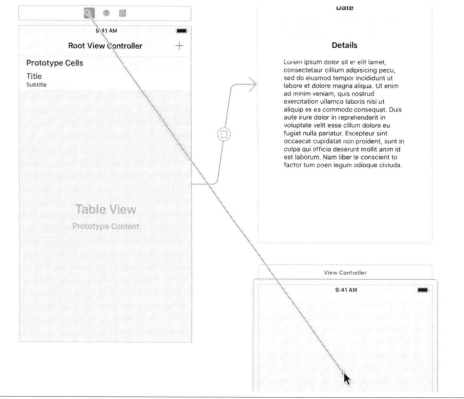

Figure 12-5

Select this segue to be a show segue so that the navigation bar on the item details view controller automatically displays a "back" button to return to the root view controller. The back button also dynamically changes depending on the title of the navigation bar on the root: try changing the title of the root view controller to "To-Do List" to see the show segue update the item details controller.

On the item details view, add five labels and a text view. Three of the labels should be sub-headers like the "Title," "Date," and "Details" labels on the other view controller. The other two will display the uneditable information (title and date), just as the text fields did in our previous controller.

Using your knowledge of constraints and UI design, lay these six components out on the view controller to look similar to *Figure 12-6*. Remember all components must have vertical and horizontal constraints of some sort, whether the bounds be width/height or item bounds.

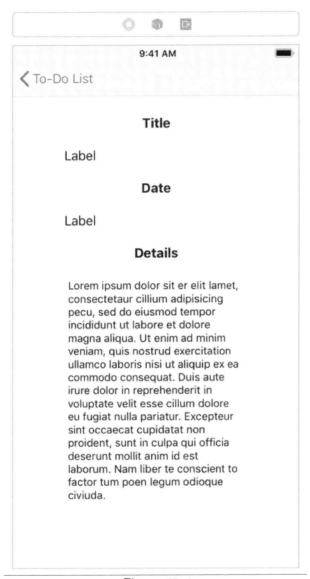

Figure 12-6

Creating .swift Files

After creating each of the three view controllers, we need to create .swift files that correspond to each of them, as the default ViewController.swift file and its corresponding storyboard object were deleted.

Since we are not customizing or programming the navigation controller, it does not require a file. For the root view controller and other two controllers, however, we need to create a TableViewController.swift file and two ViewController.swift files.

Using the main Xcode menu, navigate to File>New>File... (or press **Command** ⌘ and the **N** key). From here, select the iOS category and choose a new source file of type "Cocoa Touch Class." Change the "Subclass of" option to be `UITableViewController` and name the file `TodoListTableViewController`.

Class:	TodoListTableViewController
Subclass of:	UITableViewController
	☐ Also create XIB file
Language:	Swift

Figure 12-7

Save/create the new file to the default directory that Xcode displays.

The file has now been created, but we need to specify to the Root Table View Controller that this file is its `.swift` file. To do so, navigate to the storyboard and select the Root View Controller. Make sure the entire controller is selected, not just the table view (you can confirm this by clicking on the header for the view controller). Then, using the utility pane, navigate to the Identity Inspector tab (third icon).

Here, the dropdown menu should have a gray text which says `UITableViewController`. If the placeholder value is `UITableView`, `TableViewCell`, or `NavigationItem`, then the entire table view controller has not been selected. Use the dropdown menu to select `TodoListTableViewController` as the view controller's class:

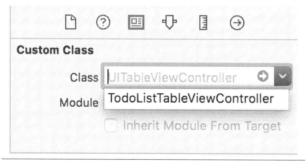

Figure 12-8

The module name should appear with a placeholder value of `To_Do_List` or whatever you set the name of the project to be.

Figure 12-9

Repeat the same steps for the next two View Controllers, naming the files `NewItemViewController` and `DetailsViewController`.

Remember that these two files must be `UIViewController` files, not `UITableViewController`!

Adding List Items to Storage

Before showing any items in the table view, the app needs to have items available in its storage to display. We will need to program the function that adds new list items to the app storage.

The first thing to do, as with every view controller, is connect each component from the storyboard to the Swift file. Using the assistant editor, create an outlet connection for the text view and two text fields from the storyboard, naming them `detailsTextView`, `titleTextField`, and `dateTextField` respectively.

```
13        @IBOutlet weak var titleTextField: UITextField!
14        @IBOutlet weak var dateTextField: UITextField!
15        @IBOutlet weak var detailsTextView: UITextView!
```

Also, add the cancel and done buttons as action functions called `cancel()` and `done()`. The placement of these functions does not matter as long as they are in the `NewItemViewController` class.

Setting Up the Basics

In the view controller, we will start with basic setup including ensuring the text fields and text view are initially blank and the cancel button works. Since the text fields and text view must be blank at the start of the app, set their `text` value to a blank `String` or `nil` in the `viewDidLoad()` function, which is called when the view controller loads the view.

Double-check that your `viewDidLoad()` function looks like the following:

```
16  override func viewDidLoad() {
17          super.viewDidLoad()
18          titleTextField.text = "" // or nil
19          dateTextField.text = ""
20          detailsTextView.text = ""
21  }
```

To make the view disappear/revert back to the root view controller when pressing cancel, use a function called `dismiss`. The `dismiss` function is used primarily for view controllers that are presented modally from another controller. Since the `NewItemViewController` was segued through a "Present Modally" segue, it technically lies <u>on top of</u> the previous controller (this is not the case for show segues). Thus, for the view controller class to remove itself as a layer, we need to use `self.dismiss()`.

 Using the keyword `self` is actually optional, as the class already knows that the `dismiss` function refers to itself. However, it is good coding practice to use the `self` keyword, as there may be certain situations where certain function handlers create ambiguity.

Upon typing `self.dismiss` into the `cancel()` function, the auto-complete feature will reveal the full function call. In the parameters list, set the `animated` parameter to be `true` and the `completion` parameter to `nil`. The `completion` parameter does not accept a variable type but rather accepts a completion handler, which is a block of code that is called after the `dismiss` action is completed.

```
23  @IBAction func cancel(_ sender: Any) {
24          self.dismiss(animated: true, completion: nil)
25  }
```

Temporarily Storing Input Values

The permanent storage feature in Swift works by having a specified key for any object stored, which is kept in the iOS device (similar to a dictionary). Since the title, date, and details of each item should be kept together, each of the input values from the `NewItemViewController` will first have to be stored temporarily in a local variable and then be grouped in a dictionary. Create respective `title`, `date`, and `details` variables for each of the `.text` values of the text fields. The local variables should be defined in the `done()` function, so that they are stored when the user presses "Done."

```
28          let title = titleTextField.text
29          let date = dateTextField.text
30          let details = detailsTextView.text
```

We only want to store the `title`, `date`, and `details` values if they are not `nil`, so add an `if` statement that only runs if `title`, `date`, **and** `details` are not `nil`.

```
32   if title != nil && date != nil && details != nil {
33          //
34   }
```

Then, in the `if` block, create a `[String:String]` dictionary which contains the values of the same three variables. The dictionary keys can be the same as the variable names. Since dictionary is temporary (will eventually be passed into permanent storage), the name is unimportant.

```
33          let itemValues = ["title": title, "date": date, "details": details]
```

Permanently Storing Values

For permanently storing values in Swift, there are two main options: core data and `NSUserDefaults`. Each method has its advantages and disadvantages concerning ease, capability, and speed. Usually, in most high-performing apps, core data always wins because of its storage capabilities and speed by which data can be accessed. However, core data (which is actually an option you can select when creating the app) is relatively difficult to learn. Since we only want to store a few simple String values, `NSUserDefaults` will be of better use for us.

`NSUserDefaults` is a default framework in the Swift language, which helps users save specific information on apps that would otherwise be removed from the application memory. For instance, whenever a user sees his/her username "autofill" in an application, the app is simply pulling the last valid username from a class in `NSUserDefaults` (if there is one) and putting it into the application. Without `NSUserDefaults`, applications wouldn't be able to save usernames and passwords, so users would have to log in each time an app is opened. In our case, we will be using the framework to save our to-do list items, so that our table view doesn't reset (erase) its values every time the app is reopened.

The syntax for using `NSUserDefaults` to store a value permanently is the following:

```
UserDefaults.standard.set(someValue, forKey: "someKey")
```

To access a stored value of a specific type, you can use the specified functions called `string()`, `int()`, `bool()`, `dictionary()`, or use the generic `object()` function:

```
UserDefaults.standard.object(forKey: "someKey")
```

Your first inclination to permanently storing the `itemValues` dictionary might be to use the `set()` function to assign a specified key to hold the `itemValues` dictionary. Initially, we won't have any values stored in the app's permanent storage, so, after adding the first to-do item, the permanent storage would hold its respective dictionary values.

However, we must consider when the permanent storage is not empty. If our specified key already contained an assigned object, then the `set()` function would replace the object, rather than add to it.

The solution to this problem is to use an array as the permanently stored object. Since arrays sequentially contain objects with numbered keys, the `append()` function can be used to add new list-items.

 Don't get confused between the array and the dictionaries we are using. The array will contain nested dictionaries, where each array object represents a list item and the list item's details are found in a nested dictionary (*Figure 12-10*).

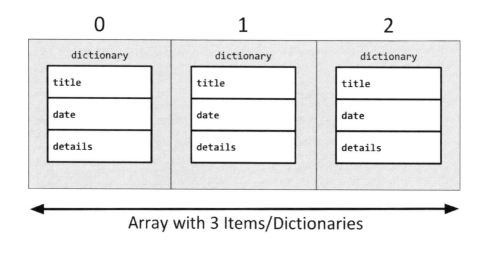

Figure 12-10

To access all of the existing items in the list, use the `.array()` function with key `"list"`. At first, this may seem odd, since we haven't even defined any object to be stored with key `"list"`. However, the function will just return an empty array if no value exists. If this is the case, we add a nil coalescer to make sure that there is a default array with no values (not to be confused with a `nil` array). At some point, however, the function will return a non-empty array with embedded dictionaries as its values. Since the array will be temporarily modified by appending the new list item to it, set the function call equal to a variable called `todoList`.

```
1        var todoList = UserDefaults.standard.array(forKey: "list") ?? []
```

Then, `append()` the `itemValues` dictionary:

```
1        todoList.append(itemValues)
```

Then, use `set()` to upload the updated `todoList` to the permanent storage with the same reference key `"list"`:

```
36        UserDefaults.standard.set(todoList, forKey: "list")
```

After pressing the "done" button and saving a new item to the list, the view controller should dismiss and return the user back to the main screen:

```
38        self.dismiss(animated: true, completion: nil)
```

Showing Items in Table Views

To show the items on the main controller (root of the navigation controller), navigate to the `TodoListTableViewController.swift` file. Similar to the previous app where we made a view controller inherit from a delegate class, this `TodoListTableView` class automatically inherits from the `UITableViewDelegate` class and `UITableViewDataSource`, which provides the necessary functions to handle the content of the table view.

Table views handle setup in three main steps:

1. First, the table view controller sets the number of sections the table view should have (specified as a return value in `numberOfSections()` function).
2. Second, the controller runs a function called `tableView(...numberOfRowsInSection...)` multiple times, depending on the number of sections specified in step one. For each function run, the function will return the respective number of rows in the section.
3. For each row in the table view, the controller runs another `tableView(...cellForRowAt...)` function, which returns the table view cell that should be created in the specified row.

Setting Number of Sections and Rows

Since our app only has one section of to-do items, the return value for the `numberOfSections()` function should be 1. The function should be defined by default in the table view controller class.

Then, using the number of list items stored in `UserDefaults`, set the return value of the `tableView(...numberOfRowsInSection...)` function.

To retrieve the number of list items, use the `UserDefaults.standard.array()` function with specified key `"list"` and set it equal to a local variable in the function (remember to add a default value since it could be `nil`). Because there is only one section in the app, we won't have to specify different return types for different values of the `section` parameter. Thus, return the `.count` attribute of the `UserDefaults` `"list"` array.

Steps 1 and 2 of the table view setup should result in the following modification of functions:

```
30  override func numberOfSections(in tableView: UITableView) -> Int {
31        return 1
32  }
33
34  override func tableView(_ tableView: UITableView, numberOfRowsInSection section: Int\
35  ) -> Int {
36        let list = UserDefaults.standard.array(forKey: "list") ?? []
37        return list.count
38  }
```

Setting Table View Cell Values

Finally, to set the value of table view cells in each row, use the `tableView(...cellForRowAt...)` function. The function is already defined in the table view controller like the previous two functions. This one, however, has to simply be uncommented without using it. Within the class, underneath the `tableView` function for `numberOfRowsInSection`, uncomment `cellForRowAt`:

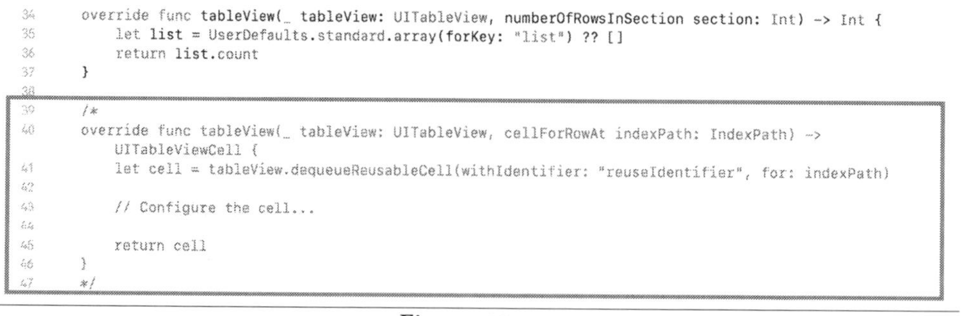

```
34  override func tableView(_ tableView: UITableView, numberOfRowsInSection section: Int) -> Int {
35        let list = UserDefaults.standard.array(forKey: "list") ?? []
36        return list.count
37  }
38
39  /*
40  override func tableView(_ tableView: UITableView, cellForRowAt indexPath: IndexPath) ->
        UITableViewCell {
41        let cell = tableView.dequeueReusableCell(withIdentifier: "reuseIdentifier", for: indexPath)
42
43        // Configure the cell...
44
45        return cell
46  }
47  */
```

Figure 12-11

On the first line of the function, a `UITableViewCell` object is initialized from a `dequeReusableCell` function, which retrieves a cell class from the storyboard and initializes it for a specific row. Since a storyboard may contain multiple prototype cells, each cell that is created must reference a prototype identifier to specify which cell it is an object of. Additionally, the cell is assigned to a specified row on the table view through its indexPath. As the function runs multiple times, it will change the parameter for indexPath, which can be used to assign the cell to a specified row and change its attributes depending on its index.

We have not yet defined a reusable identifier for the prototype table view cell created in the storyboard. Navigate to the storyboard and select the prototype cell we created on the TodoListTableView (do not select the entire table view nor just the view inside the cell). In the attributes inspector, change the "Identifier" attribute name to "listCell."

Navigating back to the Swift file, pass the identifier string "listCell" into the dequeueReusableCell initializing function.

We have now specified the table view to create a cell for each row it has and for that cell to be an object of the storyboard prototype. To specify what the text labels should display on the cell, we can retrieve the array values from UserDefaults. Then, for each cell, the row number (which starts at 0, just like an array) can be used as the index value for the stored list array (See *Figure 12-12*).

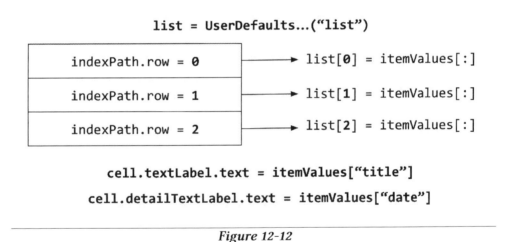

Figure 12-12

The first step is to retrieve the list array from UserDefaults by specifying the storage key and assigning it to a local variable in the function:

```
42        let list = UserDefaults.standard.array(forKey: "list") ?? []
```

Then, using the row attribute of the function's indexPath parameter, retrieve the dictionary containing the list item's values (title, date, details). Assign this to a local variable as well, force-casting the item as a [String:String] dictionary:

```
43        let itemValues = list[indexPath.row] as! [String: String]
```

When a data object is stored into UserDefaults, its variable type becomes ambiguous. Thus, when we retrieve the data again, we must use the array function to specify that the list data is stored in an array. However, since the data was ambiguous, the compiler does not know what variable type the array stores. Thus, since we know that the array stores item values in a [String:String] dictionary, that type must be specified when being accessed.

Finally, the main text label and the subtitle text label in the cell can have their text values assigned to the item dictionary's title and date attributes.

```
44          cell.textLabel?.text = itemValues["title"]
45          cell.detailTextLabel?.text = itemValues["date"]
```

The last part of the function is to return this customized cell to be passed to the function, which is already implemented:

```
47          return cell
```

Deleting Table View Cells

After programming a place for our to-do list to be displayed and a controller for new items to be added to the list, we need functionality to delete list items after they have been completed. The most efficient place to have such functionality is in the root table view controller. :uckily, table view controllers in Swift already have built-in functionality to handle deleting table view cells.

In each table view controller, table view rows can be deleted in two ways. First, as seen in several native iOS Applications such as Messages or Mail, users can swipe left on a table view to activate the delete functionality on that row. The alternate, and more common, option is to press an "edit" button, which sets the entire table view into "edit" mode in which the cells can be deleted.

For either of these options to work, the table view cells must be editable. Again, the table view controller has a function it runs for each cell to set it as editable or uneditable. Underneath the tableView(...cellForRowAt...) function, there is a commented tableView(...canEditRowAt...) function. Uncomment the function and double-check that the function has a simple return true statement in it. This ensures that every cell in our list will be deletable:

```
49  // Override to support conditional editing of the table view.
50  override func tableView(_ tableView: UITableView, canEditRowAt indexPath: IndexPath)\
51    -> Bool {
52          return true
53  }
```

Next, to support both methods of deleting, an "edit" button must be added to the navigation bar at the top of the table view controller. However, instead of creating a custom "edit" button, Swift supplies an edit button with the required functionality. In the viewDidLoad() setup function, write the following line to make an "edit" button appear on the left side of the top navigation bar:

```
15   override func viewDidLoad() {
16           super.viewDidLoad()
17           self.navigationItem.leftBarButtonItem = self.editButtonItem
18   }
```

 This line of code already appears in the viewDidLoad() function, except that it is commented out. It also sets the rightBarButtonItem equal to the editButtonItem, but since our right-side item is already the "add a new item" button, we must specify it to be the left-side item.

If we run our app now, it will display an "edit" button in the top left. However, upon pressing delete, the table view does not update. To perform this task, uncomment the tableView(...commit editingStyle...) function on the file. In this function, you'll notice an if-else if statement, in which the first if handles an edit with the .delete style, and the second else if handles an .insert edit. Since we are only concerned with deletion, delete the second else if statement.

```
51   // Override to support editing the table view.
52   override func tableView(_ tableView: UITableView, commit editingStyle: UITableViewCe\
53   llEditingStyle, forRowAt indexPath: IndexPath) {
54           if editingStyle == .delete {
55                   // Delete the row from the data source
56                   tableView.deleteRows(at: [indexPath], with: .fade)
57           }
58   }
```

With this function implemented, the table view will now delete any row that has its delete button pressed. However, this deletion will only be temporary. Every time the table view reloads, that row will reappear, as the UserDefaults storage still contains the information for that list item. Thus, above the tableView.deleteRows() function, we need to retrieve the UserDefaults array with the list, remove the list item for the corresponding row, and re-upload the edited array. Use the array remove(at: Int) function with indexPath.row as the specified array index:

```
52   override func tableView(_ tableView: UITableView, commit editingStyle: UITableViewCe\
53   llEditingStyle, forRowAt indexPath: IndexPath) {
54           if editingStyle == .delete {
55                   var list = UserDefaults.standard.array(forKey: "list") ?? []
56                   list.remove(at: indexPath.row)
57                   UserDefaults.standard.set(list, forKey: "list")
58
59                   tableView.deleteRows(at: [indexPath], with: .fade)
60           }
61   }
```

Reloading the Table View

After deleting rows in the table view controller, the table view will automatically reload with the updated table view. However, when adding items to the table view or whenever a user returns from a previous view controller to this one, there is no functionality to ensure the table will be fully updated. Thus, the final (and very short) step in this controller file is to implement the `tableView.reloadData()` function.

Normally, it would be a good idea to implement this function in the `viewDidLoad()` function, as we want the table to update once the view controller has been set up and loaded. However, after we add new items to `UserDefaults` or return from another view controller to this one, the `viewDidLoad()` function will not be called, as the view has already been loaded. Rather, another function `viewDidAppear()` will be called. It is within this function that we should reload the table view's data.

Since the `viewDidAppear()` function is not already defined in this class, we can `override` it from its superclass, as so:

```
18   override func viewDidAppear(_ animated: Bool) {
19   }
```

Then, within the function, add the reload call:

```
18   override func viewDidAppear(_ animated: Bool) {
19           tableView.reloadData()
20   }
```

Viewing Item Details

Segueing to the Details Controller

The third component of the application will be viewing item details for a to-do item whenever a user taps on a table view row. To facilitate the transition from the table view controller to the details view controller, we already set a segue between the two objects. However, this segue was not explicitly defined like the one which transitions to the new item view controller. Because the table view rows have not been initialized before the application is launched, we did not define an explicit segue, such as the one activated by a button. Thus, when a table view row is tapped, a function must be called to perform the defined segue to the destination (details view controller).

The segue will only perform once a table view row is selected, so we should retrieve the `tableView(...didSelectRowAt...)` function from the table view superclass and override it, adding in the necessary segue function.

Using the Xcode autocomplete feature, add the following `tableView()` function to the `TodoList` table view controller class:

```
65   override func tableView(_ tableView: UITableView, didSelectRowAt indexPath: IndexPat\
66   h) {
67           //
68   }
```

Make sure the compiler autocompletes the didSelectRowAt function, **not** the didDeselectRowAt function.

In the function, we need to call self.performSegue(), which takes in two parameters, withIdentifier, and sender. The sender function can simply be set to self, as the table view controller itself is activating the segue. However, we have not defined an identifier for the segue. Navigating to the storyboard, select the segue that leads from the root table view controller to the details view controller (do not select the other segue). Upon pressing it, use the attributes inspector on the right to change its "Identifier" value to showDetails.

Navigating back to our Swift file, add the following segue function to the tableView didSelectRowAt function:

```
65   override func tableView(_ tableView: UITableView, didSelectRowAt indexPath: IndexPat\
66   h) {
67           self.performSegue(withIdentifier: "showDetails", sender: self)
68   }
```

The table view will now segue to the DetailsViewController whenever any of its rows is tapped. However, we never specified which row was pressed, so the details controller has no way of knowing which list item it should display information for.

To pass that information through the segue, uncomment (or define) the prepare(for segue:) function at the bottom of the file. In the function, add an if statement to check whether the segue.identifier is equal to "showDetails":

```
69   override func prepare(for segue: UIStoryboardSegue, sender: Any?) {
70           if segue.identifier == "showDetails" {
71                   //
72           }
73   }
```

In this prepare() function, we will get the instance of the DetailsViewController that the application will segue to and pass the index of the list item to the object. That way, it can use the index to retrieve the item and its information from permanent storage. However, in order to pass the index, our DetailsViewController class must define some sort of class variable that will store this value.

Thus, navigate to the DetailsViewController.swift file. One the very first level below the class definition (not outside the class, not within a function), define a variable called selectedIndex and give it an optional integer type—do not give it an initial value, just set the type:

```
11   class DetailsViewController: UIViewController {
12
13        var selectedIndex: Int?
14
15        override func viewDidLoad() {...}
16        ...
17
18   }
```

 The selectedIndex variable is optional since we did not give it an initial value. Without this initial value, it is nil, which is only acceptable of optionals.

Simple! Going back to the table view, we need to access the instance of DetailsViewController that the app is segueing to. This can be accessed and stored in a variable—call it detailsVC and set it equal to segue.destination:

```
71               let detailsVC = segue.destination
```

However, since our code does not know what class type destination is (since there may be multiple segues), we must cast detailsVC to its respective type to access its selectedIndex variable:

```
71               let detailsVC = segue.destination as! DetailsViewController
```

The last step in the process is to set detailsVC.selectedIndex equal to the row attribute of the selected cell's index path, which can be retrieved as the .indexPathForSelectedRow attribute from the tableView.

```
69   override func prepare(for segue: UIStoryboardSegue, sender: Any?) {
70        if segue.identifier == "showDetails" {
71             let detailsVC = segue.destination as! DetailsViewController
72             detailsVC.selectedIndex = tableView.indexPathForSelectedRow?.row
73        }
74   }
```

Displaying Values

As always, connect each of the necessary components from the storyboard file to the Details View Controller. In this case, each of the three components (two labels and one text view) must be added as Outlet connections.

```
15        @IBOutlet weak var titleLabel: UILabel!
16        @IBOutlet weak var dateLabel: UILabel!
17        @IBOutlet weak var detailsTextView: UITextView!
```

Then, in the `viewDidLoad()` function, retrieve the specified item values for the selected list item. The array for "list" must first be set as a variable and then the `[String:String]` dictionary extracted with the index:

```
22        let list = UserDefaults.standard.array(forKey: "list") ?? []
23        let itemValues = list[selectedIndex!] as! [String: String]
```

Finally, the `text` attributes for each of the three components can be set using the dictionary key values.

```
25        titleLabel.text = itemValues["title"]
26        dateLabel.text = itemValues["date"]
27        detailsTextView.text = itemValues["details"]
```

The to-do list app is complete!

Extras

As an extra challenge, try and see if you can add an "edit" functionality in the app to allow users to edit their to-do items after they have been created. In this scenario, if users enable edit mode (by pressing the "edit" button), they can tap on the table view to change an item's values.

If you're stuck, here are a couple of hints:

1) You'll need to create a new view controller where users can edit their items (this one can look like the view controller where users add new items). This view controller should have editable components, like editable text fields and an editable text view.

2) In the `tableView didSelectRowAtIndexPath` function, you'll need to call a different segue depending on whether the user is in editing mode or not:

```
1  override func tableView(tableView: UITableView, didSelectRowAtIndexPath indexPath: N\
2  SIndexPath) {
3          if tableView.editing {
4                  // performSegueWithIdentifier
5                  // edit view controller
6          } else {
7                  // performSegueWithIdentifier
8                  // details view controller
9          }
10 }
```

3) Remember to account for this extra possible segue in the perform() function:

```
1  override func prepare(for segue: UIStoryboardSegue, sender: Any?) {
2          if segue.identifier == "showDetails" {
3                  let detailsVC = segue.destination as! DetailsViewController
4                  detailsVC.selectedIndex = tableView.indexPathForSelectedRow?.row
5          } else if segue.identifier = "editDetails" {
6                  // initiate the destination controller
7                  // pass the selected index, just as we did for details VC
8          }
9  }
```

4) The edit view controller must have a global variable called "selectedIndex" or else the code on Step 3 will not be able to pass the table view's index path.

5) In the edit view controller, you'll set the text values for the text fields and text view to the values for that to-do item. These can be found in NSUserDefaults using the table view selectedIndex (passed through Step 3). This is the same process as what we did in the DetailsViewController.

6) Once the user presses "Done" on the edit view controller (create a button action function for this if you haven't already), save those values to NSUserDefaults, just as we did in the NewItemViewController. However, instead of appending the item values to an array, use the selectedIndex to change the value:

```
1   @IBAction func done(_ sender: Any) {
2           let title = titleTextField.text
3           let date = dateTextField.text
4           let details = detailsTextView.text
5
6           if title != nil && date != nil && details != nil {
7                   let itemValues = ["title": title, "date": date, "details": details]
8                   var todoList = UserDefaults.standard.array(forKey: "list") ?? []
9
10                  // this is the line we changed for editing
11                  todoList[selectedIndex!] = itemValues
12
13                  UserDefaults.standard.set(todoList, forKey: "list")
14
15                  // return back to the main table view controller
16                  self.dismiss(animated: true, completion: nil)
17          }
18  }
```

Chapter Summary

Great job completing your fourth application! By learning to use table views and permanent storage, you've upped your game in going from zero to iOS hero. In addition to table views, Swift also has other types of views, such as collection views, which use the same principles of app development learned in this chapter. In addition, even though Swift Core Data is more advanced than UserDefaults, the principles we covered are at its core. These advanced concepts are applied in many of Apple's Swift documentation types, so you've learned more than just these two features.

Project Source Code

`TodoListTableViewController.swift`

```
 9  import UIKit
10
11  class TodoListTableViewController: UITableViewController {
12
13      override func viewDidLoad() {
14          super.viewDidLoad()
15          self.navigationItem.leftBarButtonItem = self.editButtonItem
16      }
17
18      override func viewDidAppear(_ animated: Bool) {
19          tableView.reloadData()
20      }
21
22      override func didReceiveMemoryWarning() {
23          super.didReceiveMemoryWarning()
24          // Dispose of any resources that can be recreated.
25      }
26
27      // MARK: - Table view data source
28
29      override func numberOfSections(in tableView: UITableView) -> Int {
30          return 1
31      }
32
33      override func tableView(_ tableView: UITableView, numberOfRowsInSection section:\
34  Int) -> Int {
35          let list = UserDefaults.standard.array(forKey: "list") ?? []
36          return list.count
37      }
38
39
40      override func tableView(_ tableView: UITableView, cellForRowAt indexPath: IndexP\
41  ath) -> UITableViewCell {
42          let cell = tableView.dequeueReusableCell(withIdentifier: "listCell", for: in\
43  dexPath)
44          let list = UserDefaults.standard.array(forKey: "list") ?? []
45          let itemValues = list[indexPath.row] as! [String: String]
46          cell.textLabel?.text = itemValues["title"]
```

```
47          cell.detailTextLabel?.text = itemValues["date"]
48
49          return cell
50      }
51
52      // Override to support conditional editing of the table view.
53      override func tableView(_ tableView: UITableView, canEditRowAt indexPath: IndexP\
54  ath) -> Bool {
55          return true
56      }
57
58
59      // Override to support editing the table view.
60      override func tableView(_ tableView: UITableView, commit editingStyle: UITableVi\
61  ewCellEditingStyle, forRowAt indexPath: IndexPath) {
62          if editingStyle == .delete {
63              var list = UserDefaults.standard.array(forKey: "list") ?? []
64              list.remove(at: indexPath.row)
65              UserDefaults.standard.set(list, forKey: "list")
66              tableView.deleteRows(at: [indexPath], with: .fade)
67          }
68      }
69
70      override func tableView(_ tableView: UITableView, didSelectRowAt indexPath: Inde\
71  xPath) {
72          self.performSegue(withIdentifier: "showDetails", sender: self)
73      }
74
75      override func prepare(for segue: UIStoryboardSegue, sender: Any?) {
76          if segue.identifier == "showDetails" {
77              let detailsVC = segue.destination as! DetailsViewController
78              detailsVC.selectedIndex = tableView.indexPathForSelectedRow?.row
79          }
80      }
81
82  }
```

NewItemViewController.swift

```
9   import UIKit
10
11  class NewItemViewController: UIViewController {
12
13      @IBOutlet weak var titleTextField: UITextField!
14      @IBOutlet weak var dateTextField: UITextField!
15      @IBOutlet weak var detailsTextView: UITextView!
16      override func viewDidLoad() {
17          super.viewDidLoad()
18          titleTextField.text = "" //or nil
19          dateTextField.text = ""
20          detailsTextView.text = ""
21      }
22
23      @IBAction func cancel(_ sender: Any) {
24          self.dismiss(animated: true, completion: nil)
25      }
26
27      @IBAction func done(_ sender: Any) {
28          let title = titleTextField.text
29          let date = dateTextField.text
30          let details = detailsTextView.text
31
32          if title != nil && date != nil && details != nil {
33              let itemValues = ["title": title, "date": date, "details": details]
34              var todoList = UserDefaults.standard.array(forKey: "list") ?? []
35              todoList.append(itemValues)
36              UserDefaults.standard.set(todoList, forKey: "list")
37
38              self.dismiss(animated: true, completion: nil)
39          }
40
41      }
42
43      override func didReceiveMemoryWarning() {
44          super.didReceiveMemoryWarning()
45          // Dispose of any resources that can be recreated.
46      }
47  }
```

DetailsViewController.swift

```
 9   import UIKit
10
11   class DetailsViewController: UIViewController {
12
13       var selectedIndex: Int?
14
15       @IBOutlet weak var titleLabel: UILabel!
16       @IBOutlet weak var dateLabel: UILabel!
17       @IBOutlet weak var detailsTextView: UITextView!
18
19       override func viewDidLoad() {
20           super.viewDidLoad()
21
22           let list = UserDefaults.standard.array(forKey: "list") ?? []
23           let itemValues = list[selectedIndex!] as! [String: String]
24
25           titleLabel.text = itemValues["title"]
26           dateLabel.text = itemValues["date"]
27           detailsTextView.text = itemValues["details"]
28
29       }
30
31       override func didReceiveMemoryWarning() {
32           super.didReceiveMemoryWarning()
33           // Dispose of any resources that can be recreated.
34       }
35
36   }
```

Chapter Thirteen: Web Content and Data (App #5)

Introduction

One of the best technologies in Xcode and the Swift Development Kit is the WebKit View, which allows for apps to gain functionality with embedded web content and navigation. In the Swift language, accessibility to web data already exists, but WebKit View allows for that data to be displayed in apps.

To learn to use and integrate this feature in our applications, we will create a simple web browser application, in which the user can navigate to a website and view its contents on the phone screen (essentially a web browser). In addition, the user will also be able to view the HTML or JSON data content presented on the requested URL.

In addition to the visual web content on the WebKit View using Swift web features, the ability for iOS devices to access data content on webpages is the core functionality that WebKit provides. Later in the chapter, we'll use a short Playground program to explore how web content (mainly JSON) can be transformed into information that you can use in creating more powerful apps.

Using the WebKit View

Setup

Open a new Xcode Project called "Web Content." On the Main.Storyboard file, add a WebKit View (not a "Web View," which will say "deprecated"), as well as a Search Bar. Rearrange the two components so that the search bar is constrained to the top and sides, and the WebKit View is constrained to the bottom of the screen and sides below the search bar, as in *Figure 13-1*:

Figure 13-1

Opening up the assistant editor, connect the two components with identifiers searchBar and webView.

 The webKit outlet will appear with an error message (*Figure 13-2*). Since WebKit components are not a part of the default UIKit library present on Swift view controllers, the WebKit library needs to be imported into the ViewControler.swift file.

```
 9 import UIKit
10 class ViewController: UIViewController {
11
⊙       @IBOutlet weak var webView: WKWebView!   ❗ Use of undeclared type 'WKWebView'
⊙       @IBOutlet weak var searchBar: UISearchBar!
14
```

Figure 13-2

Above the class definition, place an `import` statement for `WebKit` alongside the `UIKit` statement:

```
 9 import UIKit
10 import WebKit
```

The search bar in the application will also need the class to be assigned as its delegate, just like the table view in Chapter 12. First, add `UISearchBarDelegate` to the class definition:

```
11 class ViewController: UIViewController, UISearchBarDelegate { ... }
```

Then, in the `viewDidLoad()` function, set the `searchBar` component's `delegate` value equal to the current class:

```
16 override func viewDidLoad() {
17        super.viewDidLoad()
18        searchBar.delegate = self
19 }
```

Searching Using the WebKit View

Any time a user presses the "Search" button on the Search bar's keyboard, the application should search for whatever the user typed in the search engine. To facilitate this process, we first need a function that is run whenever the "Search" button is pressed. After setting the class to be a `UISearchBarDelegate`, the following function will be available to define (either manually or using auto-complete) in the Swift file:

```
21 func searchBarSearchButtonClicked(_ searchBar: UISearchBar) {
22        //
23 }
```

The first step is to store the searchBar.text attribute as a variable (with nil coalescing to handle blank values):

```
21   func searchBarSearchButtonClicked(_ searchBar: UISearchBar) {
22          let searchText = searchBar.text ?? " "
23   }
```

 Notice that when referencing searchBar in the function, you refer to the function parameter searchBar: UISearchBar in the function definition, not the global one in the class definition. This is due to how Swift handles scope, discussed in the previous section. However, since there is only one search bar in the application, these two references both reference the same search bar, so both self.searchBar.text and searchBar.text are accurate.

The search engine used for this demonstration will be Google.

We'll use the URL https://www.google.com/search?q=, followed by a string value of what we want Google to search for. However, since URLs naturally cannot have strings in them, Google uses plus characters (+) between each search keyword in the URL. For instance, if we want to search for "best iOS programming book", our string will be "best+iOS+programming+book". To do so, we'll use the String .replacingOccurences function to generate the joined String and store it in another variable:

```
23          let urlSearchText = searchText.replacingOccurrences(of: " ", with: "+")
```

Then, we will concatenate the base Google search URL with urlSearchText to form the final URL for the WebKit View. This can either be done by adding the two Strings together:

```
24          let urlString = "https://www.google.com/search?q=" + urlSearchText
```

Or, more intuitively (and preferrably), using **String interpolation** and using the backslash escape character and parentheses to insert the value of urlSearchText into the URL, rather than adding it to the end:

```
24          let urlString = "https://www.google.com/search?q=\(urlSearchText)"
```

Using urlString, create a new URL object directed towards this URL:

```
25          let url = URL(string: urlString)
```

This URL object should then set up a URLRequest object, which handles and loads the URL object. Usually, there are many different attributes and parameters which can be changed for a URLRequest, but, for our purposes, we will use a basic implementation:

```
26          let request = URLRequest(url: url!)
```

 Since the URLRequest should guarantee successfully loading a URL, we need to put an exclamation point to confirm that the URL exists.

The final step is to have the webView load our request:

```
27          webView.load(request)
```

Running our application, we can type into the search bar on the Xcode simulator, and the webview will load the search results (*Figure 13-3*).

Figure 13-3

Other URLS on the WebKit View

WebKit Views can also handle many other URL request types in addition to those for searching on Google. As long as URLs begin with https://www., the WebKit View will be able to handle a request properly. To reduce the use of www and https while a user types URLs, the replacingOccurences function can be used to remove any extra typed protocols and add "https://www." to the front of each URL.

To illustrate the general approach to using URLs and WebKit Views:

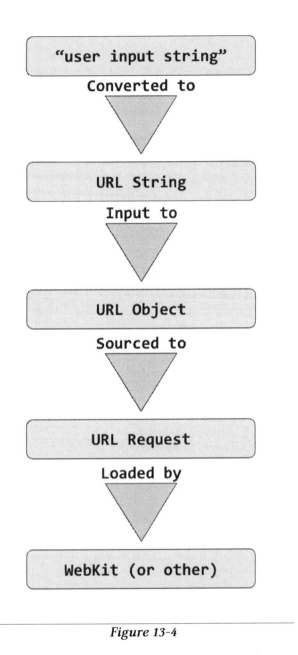

Figure 13-4

Retrieving Data Content from the Web

To demonstrate the value of retrieving web data content, open a new blank Xcode Playground. In this file, we will create a URL and a Data Session (rather than a URL Request). In the Data Session, we'll access the data content from an online JSON (JavaScript Online Notation) source and convert it into a useable dictionary that Swift projects can use.

JSON (JavaScript Object Notation) is a storage file format used by many technologies to store and transmit data. It allows for the storage of objects or arrays in key-value pairs, similar to how dictionaries store data in Swift.

The JSON web source we will use is a fake online server API (Application Protocol Interface) for testing and prototyping. However, the code written for accessing this API can be replicated for many types of APIs.

The first step in accessing an online API is creating a URL object. To do so, import WebKit into the Playground file and create a URL object using the following string:

https://jsonplaceholder.typicode.com/todos/1.

```
1  import WebKit
2
3  let url = URL(string: "https://jsonplaceholder.typicode.com/todos/1")
```

Type this URL into a web browser. Notice the JSON content on this server URL is in key value form:

Figure 13-5

This mock data is the JSON content that the URL Session will retrieve and convert into usable Swift data.

Additionally, add the following import statement at the top of the Playground beneath the import WebKit line, accompanied by the Playground attribute statement:

```
2  import PlaygroundSupport
3  PlaygroundPage.current.needsIndefiniteExecution = true
```

This line will allow the Playground to execute long enough for the data content to be retrieved from the web. Normally, an Xcode Project would not require this line, but Playgrounds have lower default timeout times, so they do not allow enough time for the server and code to communicate and transmit data.

Next, create a variable called session and set it equal to the following:

```
7   let session = URLSession.shared
```

The Playground code should now have the following five lines:

```
1   import WebKit
2   import PlaygroundSupport
3   PlaygroundPage.current.needsIndefiniteExecution = true
4
5   let url = URL(string: "https://jsonplaceholder.typicode.com/todos/1")
6
7   let session = URLSession(configuration: URLSessionConfiguration.default)
```

Similar to loading content like a URLRequest, the URLSession provides methods and protocols to download data through a "data task."

To initiate a data task from the URLSession, create a task variable equal to session.dataTask(). The dataTask() function is polymorphic and has several different forms, each with a different set of parameters. Select the dataTask() function with the with and completionHandler parameters, as shown:

Figure 13-6

For the first parameter, in the URL placeholder, reference url! as an unwrapped URL object. For the completionHandler parameter, double-click to reveal three extra parameters for the completionHandler function (Data, URLResponse and Error). Once the dataTask function is run and completed, the completionHandler function will execute. Each of the three parameters above will be retrieved from the dataTask function, so we will be able to get the web server's data and response and handle any errors that occur. For the three parameters in the completionHandler, name the variables data, response, and error, respectively:

```
9   let task = session.dataTask(with: url!) { (data, response, error) in
10          //
11  }
```

In some cases, web servers may return data as nil. Thus, use optional binding in an if statement (if let newVariable = optionalVariable) to only process non-nil data. In the optional binding statement, let's try printing out the data content:

```
 9   let task = session.dataTask(with: url!) { (data, response, error) in
10          if let content = data {
11                  print(content)
12          }
13   }
```

At first, this code will not execute in the Playground, since the task variable was <u>defined</u>, but never <u>executed</u>. By default, URLSessionDataTask types are initialized with a "suspended" state (*Figure 13-7*):

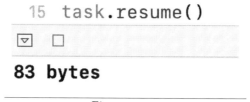

Figure 13-7

To run the data task, call task.resume() at the end of the Playground, which will change the data task status to "running" and print out the data content:

```
15   task.resume()
```

In the output section, the only information outputted about the data is its size because the raw data was not serialized from JSON:

```
15  task.resume()
```

83 bytes

Figure 13-8

Now, we want to convert this data from its original JSON form on the web into readable content, such as a dictionary, in Swift. JSON Serialization can be done in the same if statement through the JSONSerialization class's jsonObject() function, which returns a Swift-readable array or dictionary. Set this function equal to an object variable, set content for the Data parameter, and .mutableContainers for the options parameter. The .mutableContainers option specifies that the object created is mutable (dynamic), so we can edit it after it has been created.

```
10   if let content = data {
11          let object = JSONSerialization.jsonObject(with: content,
12                  options: .mutableContainers)
13   }
```

Upon this, the Playground console will receive an error message:

```
☑ ▶
Playground execution failed:

error: DataContent.playground:5:22: error: call can throw, but it is not marked with 'try' and the error is not handled
        let object = JSONSerialization.jsonObject(with: content, options: .mutableContainers)
                   ^
```

Figure 13-9

This type of error is common with many Swift advanced features and requires **error handling**. The Swift function `jsonObject()` can fail (since `content` might not be JSON convertable), but the compiler does not know how to react if there is a failure. Thus, we need to be able to catch any errors the function throws, handle those errors, and keep the program running without crashing. This is similar to how we tried to handle possible `nil` values to avoid crashing the project in previous chapters.

To perform error handling, put the error-throwing statement inside of a code block (similar to an `if` block) that begins with the word `do`:

```
11  do {
12          let object = JSONSerialization.jsonObject(with: content,
13                  options: .mutableContainers)
14  }
```

Next, place `try` in front of the function call:

```
11  do {
12          let object = try JSONSerialization.jsonObject(with: content,
13                  options: .mutableContainers)
14  }
```

Additionally, add a statement to print out the value of `object`.

Finally, add a `catch` block following the `do` block, similar to how an `else` block follows an `if` block. In the `catch` block, put a `print` statement to output that there was an error in the Playground.

```
11  do {
12          let object = try JSONSerialization.jsonObject(with: content,
13                  options: .mutableContainers)
14          print(object)
15  } catch {
16          print("There was an error.")
17  }
```

This way, if `JSONSerialization` fails, the compiler outputs a message, instead of crashing.

Now, when we run our program, the full Swift object form of the JSON is printed to the console:

```
{
    completed = 0;
    id = 1;
    title = "delectus aut autem";
    userId = 1;
}
```

Figure 13-10

We can also access specific attributes from the `object` variable, just as we do when retrieving dictionary values, as the `object` can be cast to represent a Swift dictionary object, rather than a JSON object:

```
13        let dictionary = object as! [String: Any]
14        print(dictionary["title"]!) // prints "delectus aut autem"
```

The `url` can also be changed to get different values. For instance, if we changed the `url` to be `"https://jsonplaceholder.../2"` instead of `"https://jsonplaceholder.../1"`, we could retrieve different titles, userIds, and other attributes. Similarly, we can access and process the JSON content of sites with huge amounts of data.

This basic feature of retrieving JSON content is used in almost all web applications. From Google's Blogger pages to backend databases, many websites store all of their information in JSON format, so mastering the Swift techniques to use JSON will be essential in connecting your apps to dynamic data. Combining the concepts in this chapter with things we learned about program flow and user interfaces can allow you to create very powerful apps that can process heavy amounts of JSON data quickly.

Chapter Summary

Only one more app to go. Congratulations on completing your fifth app (plus a bonus Playground)! In this app, we applied several WebKit and other Swift features, including:

- Using the WebKitView and UISearchBar
- String interpolation
- URL object Creation and running URLRequest
- Using PlaygroundSupport for server-based Playgrounds
- Initiating URLSession
- Creating a dataTask from a URL and URLSession
- Running a dataTask using the .resume() function
- Using completion handlers
- Converting JSON webdata into Swift objects/dictionaries
- Error handling (throw and catch)

Through learning these concepts and technologies, you can now use web servers and APIs to store data on the web and retrieve it in your apps. The applications are endless, from messaging to games to sharing apps and any other creative ideas you come up with. Even the largest websites, like YouTube, Google, and Wikipedia, use JSON technologies to process and store data. Using these skills, you can create apps such as Blog Reader apps. WebKit also has other protocols, in addition to URLSession and URLRequest, so that even more advanced features can be utilized, but they will use the same principles of data retrieval learned in this chapter. Rather than having a stand-alone app, these concepts will help you take your applications to the next level, accessing remote data and the web for more versatility.

Project Source Code

ViewController.swift

```swift
 9   import UIKit
10   import WebKit
11   class ViewController: UIViewController, UISearchBarDelegate {
12
13       @IBOutlet weak var webView: WKWebView!
14       @IBOutlet weak var searchBar: UISearchBar!
15
16       override func viewDidLoad() {
17           super.viewDidLoad()
18           searchBar.delegate = self
19       }
20
21       func searchBarSearchButtonClicked(_ searchBar: UISearchBar) {
22           let searchText = searchBar.text ?? " "
23           let urlSearchText = searchText.replacingOccurrences(of: " ", with: "+")
24           let urlString = "https://www.google.com/search?q=\(urlSearchText)"
25           let url = URL(string: urlString)
26           let request = URLRequest(url: url!)
27           webView.load(request)
28       }
29
30
31   }
```

DataContent.playground

```
1   import WebKit
2   import PlaygroundSupport
3   PlaygroundPage.current.needsIndefiniteExecution = true
4
5   let url = URL(string: "https://jsonplaceholder.typicode.com/todos/1")
6
7   let session = URLSession(configuration: URLSessionConfiguration.default)
8
9   let task = session.dataTask(with: url!) { (data, response, error) in
10      if let content = data {
11          do {
12              let object = try JSONSerialization.jsonObject(with: content, options: .m\
13  utableContainers)
14              let dictionary = object as! [String: Any]
15              print(dictionary["title"]!)
16          } catch {
17              print("There was an error.")
18          }
19      }
20  }
21
22  task.resume()
```

Chapter Fourteen: Maps, Geo-Location, and Alerts (App #6)

Introduction

The final Advanced Swift technologies we'll explore are the MapKit and CoreLocation frameworks (and some extra bonuses like Alert Controllers and Gestures) in Xcode. As the name suggests, the MapKit framework opens up new doors for iOS Programming by allowing users to experience a map on their screen and get dynamic location-based data through CoreLocation.

To integrate MapKit into our programming skillset, we will create an application in which a user can view a map with a specified coordinate with their own location (or the simulator's "fake" location) and add pins on their favorite map points.

Setting Up and Using MapKit

Layout

Create a new Xcode project called "Geo Location." On Main.Storyboard, add a Map Kit View and a Navigation bar to the main view controller. Add constraints to the items so that they fill the entire screen and are vertically adjacent:

Figure 14-1

On the top navigation bar, add two different buttons, one for displaying the user's current location on the map and one for displaying a specified geographic coordinate (latitude/longitude). At the center of the navigation bar, change the Title to "GeoLocation." On the left and right sides of the navigation bar, add two "Bar Button Items" called "Current" and "Custom":

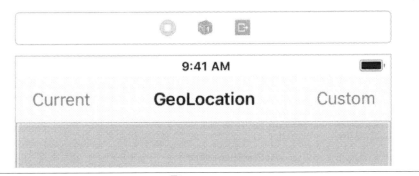

Figure 14-2

Then, connect each of the buttons as an action connection from the storyboard to the `ViewController.swift` file and connect the MapView as an outlet connection. You'll also need to import `MapKit` for the MapView to work properly:

```
14   @IBOutlet weak var map: MKMapView!
15
16   @IBAction func currentLocation(_ sender: Any) {
17         //
18   }
19
20   @IBAction func customLocation(_ sender: Any) {
21         //
22   }
```

After making the object and function references, run the simulator to ensure the `MapView` shows a default location.

Showing Locations on MapKit

The first feature of this app will be to allow users to input a custom location (latitude and longitude) for the MapView to display. When the user presses the "Custom" button, activating the `customLocation()` function, the application should display a prompt with two text fields for the user's desired latitude and longitude coordinates, like the following:

Figure 14-3

This type of prompt on an iOS application is a UIAlertController. Often times, alert controllers are used to display required information the user must understand or input to before proceeding with a function. In most cases, an alert controller won't have text fields, but, for specific cases (like the one for this app) where we need text fields, it can handle that functionality.

Creating AlertControllers

The entire alert controller and its text fields and action buttons will be created and handled in the customLocation() function. On the first line of the function, create a new variable called alert that stores a new UIAlertController object. To initialize that object, use the object definition with the following parameters (*Figure 14-4*):

Figure 14-4

Put "Custom Location," which will appear in bold at the top of the alert controller, for title. For message, put instructions, such as "Please enter your desired location." For preferred style, the alert can appear on the bottom of the screen (action sheet) or in the middle (alert). Since the middle is more accessible and appropriate for our situation, put .alert as the preferredStyle parameter:

```
24   let alert = UIAlertController(title: "Custom Location", message: "Please enter you\
25 r desired location", preferredStyle: .alert)
```

After creating the main alert, which will be the parent controller for the text fields and action buttons, we need to add two text fields and configure them. Simply type alert.addTextField to reveal a function that adds a text field:

```
alert.addTextField(configurationHandler: ((UITextField) -> Void)?)
```

Figure 14-5

This function also includes a configuration handler as a parameter, which we can use to set up the text field.

 Configuration handlers are very similar to completion handlers in that sthey represent a code block that is run after a certain function is executed. In this case, however, the configuration handler has the new text field as its only passed value, allowing for us to access and edit that text field. Completion handlers, on the other hand, have error or data values that can be accessed after the function is run.

Press enter on the configuration handler parameter to open the handler function, in which we will call our text field latitudeField. In the function, change the placeholder value of this field to be the String "Latitude" to finish this field's setup.

```
26    alert.addTextField { (latitudeField) in
27      latitudeField.placeholder = "Latitude"
28    }
```

Repeat this process to add a second text field for longitude.

The only two components remaining are the two action buttons: one to cancel (not execute the custom location) and another to confirm the coordinates.

To add the cancel action, create a new variable cancel and set it equal to a UIAlertAction. Using the default (and only) initializer, set the action title equal to "Cancel," the style equal to .cancel, and the handler as nil.

```
34    let cancel = UIAlertAction(title: "Cancel", style: .cancel, handler: nil)
```

Then, call the alert.addAction() function and pass the cancel object as the parameter:

```
35    alert.addAction(cancel)
```

Create a second UIAlertAction called confirm. Set its title to "Go" or "Confirm" and set its style equal to .default (since we do not want it to look like a cancel action button). However, do not set the handler equal to nil. Instead, open the action handler and set its parameter name to action:

```
37    let confirm = UIAlertAction(title: "Go", style: .default) { (action) in
38      //
39    }
```

This handler will execute whenever the confirm action is selected (button pressed). Thus, in this handler, we should retrieve the two text field values and set the map location. For now, leave the action handler code blank.

This `confirm` action object also must be added to the `alert` controller, so call the `alert.addAction()` function and pass the `confirm` object as the parameter:

```
40    alert.addAction(confirm)
```

Perfect. Now that both text fields and both action items have been added to the alert controller, we can ask the current view controller to present the completed `alert` object:

```
42    self.present(alert, animated: true, completion: nil)
```

We can test to make sure that the alert controller like the one in *Figure 14-3* appears when the "Custom" button is pressed in the simulator.

Setting Map Coordinates

All of the map coordinate execution will occur in the action handler of the `confirm` object, since that handler will be executed if the user presses "Go" or "Confirm."

First, we need to retrieve the values from the two text fields. When text fields are added to alerts, they are stored in an array, so the first text field we added (for latitude) will be at that array's `[0]` index, and the second one will be at the `[1]` index. We also need to check if the values are `nil` to cancel in the case of a blank field or convert the Strings to numbers if they are non-`nil`.

Thus, first check if either value is `nil`:

```
37    let confirm = UIAlertAction(title: "Go", style: .default) { (action) in
38      if let lat = alert.textFields![0].text, let long = alert.textFields![1].text {
39
40      } else {
41        // One or both text fields are nil
42        // Do Nothing
43      }
44    }
```

If both values are non-`nil`, convert the `lat` and `long` Strings to `Double` values:

```
40    let latDouble = Double(lat)
41    let longDouble = Double(long)
```

Apple's `MapKit` framework depends on locational points being expressed as `CoreLocation` types (which is another framework built into Xcode). Thus, instead of asking for `MapKit` to read `Double` types, we have to create two `CLLocationDegrees` objects that have the value of the `Double` variables.

```
43    let latitude = CLLocationDegrees(exactly: latDouble!)
44    let longitude = CLLocationDegrees(exactly: longDouble!)
```

These two can be combined into a CLLocationCoordinate2D to specify a single location point that lies at the intersection of the two coordinates:

```
46    let location = CLLocationCoordinate2DMake(latitude!, longitude!)
```

In addition to the location of a point, MapKit also needs to know the span of the location. In other words, it needs to know how "zoomed in" it should be on the location; how much land should it show around the specified point?

To specify this amount, we need to create a MapKit coordinate span, which can be done by calling MKCoordinateSpanMake(). For our purposes, we will have the span display 0.01 degrees latitudinally and 0.01 degrees longitudinally. You can try changing these values once the app has been created.

```
47    let span = MKCoordinateSpanMake(0.01, 0.01)
```

The location and span of a point can be combined to create a MapKit coordinate region (MKCoordinateRegion) object, using the following function:

```
49    let region = MKCoordinateRegionMake(location, span)
```

Finally, use the map's setRegion() function to view this location on the device. We should reference self whenever we are within a completion/configuration/action handler to reference the ViewController as a whole, since the mapView object is defined in the ViewController and **not** in the action handler:

```
49    self.map.region = region
```

Run the simulator and check it out. Try the coordinates 40.6892 for latitude and -74.0445 for the longitude. If the device shows the Statue of Liberty, then the code works! If you want to see more surrounding area, change the coordinate span values to a larger number, like 0.05 or 0.1.

GeoLocating Users

The next step is to activate the "Current" button and show the user's current location on the map.

To access the user's location, Xcode requires several steps. The first involves navigating to the main project page in Xcode (selected in *Figure 14-6*):

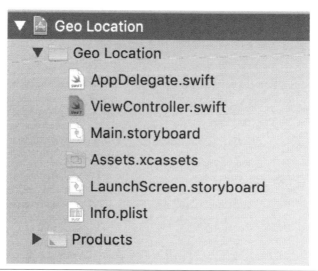

Figure 14-6

On this page, navigate to the "Build Phases" tab and under the "Link Binary with Libraries" section, press the add (+) button and add the CoreLocation framework:

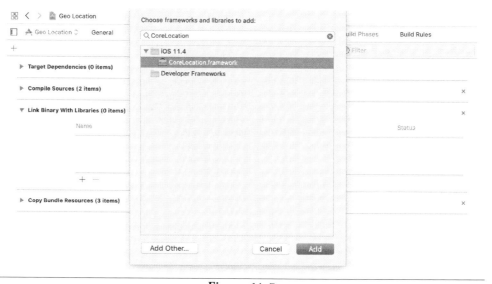

Figure 14-7

The next step is to navigate to the Info.Plist file, where all of the application permissions and core application properties are stored. There, add a new property (see *Figure 14-8*) called "Privacy - Location When In Use Usage Description" (select using the dropdown menu after creating a new property) and set its value equal to a String message like "We need to display your location on the map."

Key	Type	Value
▼ Information Property List	Dictionary	(14 items)
Localization native development re...	String	$(DEVELOPMENT_LANGUAGE)
Executable file	String	$(EXECUTABLE_NAME)
Bundle identifier	String	$(PRODUCT_BUNDLE_IDENTIFIER)
InfoDictionary version	String	6.0

Figure 14-8

This allows the application to ask for the user's location with the specified message. If the user allows for location usage, we can access the device location.

Once these two tasks have been completed, navigate back to `ViewController.swift` and in the class definition, add `CLLocationManagerDelegate`:

```
49   class ViewController: UIViewController, CLLocationManagerDelegate { ... }
```

Just as we've done for text fields and table views, this delegate is necessary for the class to access all of the functions required to use the device's location.

We'll also import `CoreLocation`:

```
9    import UIKit
10   import MapKit
11   import CoreLocation
```

The first thing you need to do is create a location manager instance. Every time we need to access the user's location, we will reference the location manager object. Define a new variable called `locationManager` and set it equal to a new instance of `CLLocationManager()`. It should be defined in the class, but <u>outside</u> of any function, so we can access it anywhere in the `ViewController` class:

```
13   class ViewController: UIViewController, CLLocationManagerDelegate {
14
15       var locationManager = CLLocationManager()
16       ...
17   }
```

In the `viewDidLoad()` method, adjust some of the settings for this `locationManager`, including setting its `delegate` equal to the `ViewController` class, setting the desired location accuracy, and requesting the user's authorization.

```
66   override func viewDidLoad() {
67          super.viewDidLoad()
68          locationManager.delegate = self
69          locationManager.desiredAccuracy = kCLLocationAccuracyBest
70          locationManager.requestWhenInUseAuthorization()
71   }
```

The first and second lines are straightforward, as we've done this for most of our applications. The third line sets the accuracy of this manager to be the best. If we wanted to simply know which region someone is in, we could use a different setting. The fourth line is important to note, however. When asking a location manager to request location use, there are two options: requestAlwaysAuthorization() and requestWhenInUserAuthorization(). The difference between these lies in whether the application can access the device's location in the background, or only when it is being used. For our purposes, we only need it when in use, but if we needed to access it all the time, the Info.Plist file would also need an additional component for the "always" authorization, just as we did for the "when in use" authorization.

Lastly, once the view has loaded and we've set up locationManager, we can start updating the user's location if the user presses the "Current" button:

```
19   @IBAction func currentLocation(_ sender: Any) {
20          locationManager.startUpdatingLocation()
21   }
```

Once the location manager starts updating the device's location, we can retrieve this location through one of the locationManager functions, which is run every time that the user registers a new location. Create a new function in the class by typing func locationManager and select the following didUpdateLocations function:

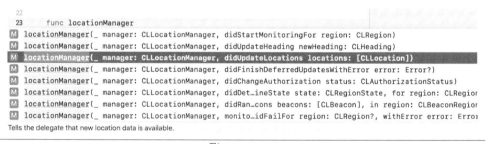

Figure 14-9

In this function, we'll try printing out the location of the user to the console. Notice the locations parameter in this function takes the form of an array ([CLLocation]). Since this function is called every time a user changes locations, there may be multiple locations registered for the user, leading to the need for the CLLocation array. However, we want to print out the first location transmitted to the location manager, so we can print locations[0]:

```
23  func locationManager(_ manager: CLLocationManager, didUpdateLocations locations: [CL\
24  Location]) {
25          print(locations[0])
26  }
```

If we run the app now, the application will request our location (*Figure 14-10*). After pressing "Current," Xcode will print out the device's current location (*Figure 14-11*). Note that since we are running this application on a simulator, it will return a simulated location, not the actual location of your computer.

Figure 14-10

```
<+37.78583400,-122.40641700> +/- 5.00m (speed -1.00 mps / course -1.00) @
11/20/18, 12:55:47 PM Mountain Standard Time
<+37.78583400,-122.40641700> +/- 5.00m (speed -1.00 mps / course -1.00) @
11/20/18, 12:55:47 PM Mountain Standard Time
<+37.78583400,-122.40641700> +/- 5.00m (speed -1.00 mps / course -1.00) @
11/20/18, 12:59:22 PM Mountain Standard Time
```

Figure 14-11

To see how the function continually updates, we can change the simulated location to a moving location by navigating to Debug>Locations>Freeway Ride on the Xcode application bar:

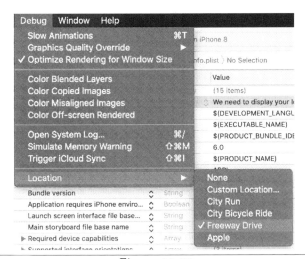

Figure 14-12

The Xcode console will now print out a continuous stream of location data, showing the simulated user's location constantly updating. This data can be used for a variety of things, but our app will only need longitude and latitude.

Navigating back to the `ViewController`, we need to show this location on `mapView`. Thus, in the `locationManager(...didUpdateLocations...)` function, create a new variable `location`:

```
25          let location = locations[0].coordinate
```

Then, using the same `span` as the custom location function, create a `region` and set it equal to the map's `region`:

```
25  func locationManager(_ manager: CLLocationManager, didUpdateLocations locations: [CL\
26  Location]) {
27          print(locations[0])
28          let location = locations[0].coordinate
29          let span = MKCoordinateSpanMake(0.1, 0.1)
30          let region = MKCoordinateRegionMake(location, span)
31          self.map.region = region
32  }
```

Finally, add the following line after setting the region to display the point with the user's location:

```
30          map.showsUserLocation = true
```

Run the app, press "Current," and the location of the simulator appears!

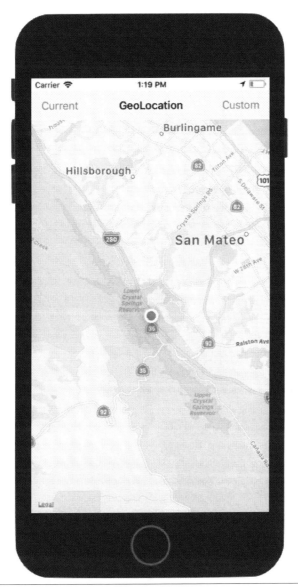

Figure 14-13

The location will also move if a non-static location is selected in the simulator "Debug" section (*Figure 14-12*).

Integrating MapKit and Pin Annotations

In addition to geolocating users and finding certain places on a MapView, the MapKit framework allows for pins (or annotations) to be added to a MapView to save certain locations:

Figure 14-14

Adding Pins on Specified Points

Adding map annotations is simple. Let's add a map annotation for the custom locations that users enter in our app. In the customLocation() function, after the last line in the action handler (where we set the map region), create a new annotation variable as a MKPointAnnotation object. This code should still be in the action handler for the confirm action object.

```
60          . . .
61          self.map.region = region
62          var annotation = MKPointAnnotation()
63          . . .
```

Then, set the title and subtitle attributes for this object. Also set the coordinate attribute for this object to location (which was the coordinate object the user specified in the custom location).

```
63          annotation.title = "Marked Location"
64          annotation.subtitle = "One of my favorite places!"
65          annotation.coordinate = location
```

Finally, use the map view's addAnnotation() function to add this annotation point:

```
66          self.map.addAnnotation(annotation)
```

Now, upon entering a custom location, you will see a location pin appear at the coordinate you inputted.

Using Gestures to Add Pins

Another way to add pins (and to perform a lot of actions) is to use gestures, such as long presses, taps, shake, etc. In many navigation apps, including Apple Maps, by long pressing on a certain point in the view, users can add a pin annotation, just as we did for the custom location. To do so, we have to add a gesture recognizer to our application.

In the viewDidLoad() method, add a new variable called longPressRecognizer and set it equal to a new instance of UILongPressGestureRecognizer() with parameters target and action. For target, put the current view controller (self), and for the action parameter, add the following expression:

#selector(addAnnotation(_:))

```
84        var longPressRecognizer = UILongPressGestureRecognizer(target: self,
85        action: #selector(addAnnotation(_:)))
```

The action parameter tells the gesture recognizer which function to call when a long press gesture is recognized and how to pass the value of that gesture to the function. Since we have no function named addAnnotation() yet, let's go ahead and create one, with a parameter of type UILongPressGestureRecognizer.

```
88   func addAnnotation(_ gestureRecognizer: UILongPressGestureRecognizer) {
89   }
```

The underscore and colon at the end of the function selector tells the gesture recognizer object to pass its value to the function as a parameter, so we need some way of handling that parameter. Thus, we have the parameter gestureRecognizer in our new function. Additionally, since we left that parameter unnamed in the selector (underscores stand for unnamed objects in Swift), we put the underscore in front of the gestureRecognizer name in the function call. This way, it retrieves the unnamed parameter and assigns it to the parameter named gestureRecognizer.

Upon doing this, the function will require @objc to be added at the front, since selectors are inherently Objective-C (pre-Swift) features.

```
90   @objc func addAnnotation(_ gestureRecognizer: UILongPressGestureRecognizer) {
91   }
```

In the viewDidLoad() method, specify the long press duration and add that gesture recognizer to our map view:

```
78  override func viewDidLoad() {
79          super.viewDidLoad()
80          locationManager.delegate = self
81          locationManager.desiredAccuracy = kCLLocationAccuracyBest
82          locationManager.requestWhenInUseAuthorization()
83
84          var longPressRecognizer = UILongPressGestureRecognizer(target: self,
85                  action: #selector(addAnnotation(_:)))
86          longPressRecognizer.minimumPressDuration = 2.0
87          map.addGestureRecognizer(longPressRecognizer)
88  }
```

Now, we can add the annotations in the addAnnotation() function. First, we'll retrieve the exact point on the screen where the user performed the long press (so that we can add the pin there). This is found by executing the location(in:) function on the gestureRecognizer with a parameter of the map view:

```
90  @objc func addAnnotation(_ gestureRecognizer: UILongPressGestureRecognizer) {
91          let point = gestureRecognizer.location(in: map)
92  }
```

The point object represents the exact point on the <u>view</u> that the user pressed, not the actual geographic coordinate where we need to add the pin. Thus, use the map view's convert(toCoordinateFrom:) function:

```
90  @objc func addAnnotation(_ gestureRecognizer: UILongPressGestureRecognizer) {
91          let point = gestureRecognizer.location(in: map)
92          let coordinate = map.convert(point, toCoordinateFrom: map)
93  }
```

Then, using the same steps we used to create our first annotation, create a new annotation with a specified title and subtitle and the coordinate of the user's press:

```
90   @objc func addAnnotation(_ gestureRecognizer: UILongPressGestureRecognizer) {
91           let point = gestureRecognizer.location(in: map)
92           let coordinate = map.convert(point, toCoordinateFrom: map)
93
94           var annotation = MKPointAnnotation()
95           annotation.title = "New Location"
96           annotation.subtitle = "Where I want to go!"
97           annotation.coordinate = coordinate
98           self.map.addAnnotation(annotation)
99   }
```

Now, long presses can create new points on the map!

Figure 14-15

You can extend this app with MapView in many more ways! Try experimenting with using UIAlertControllers to display more of the user's information, such as their latitude, longitude, speed, altitude, etc. You can also try using CLGeocoder to find the user's nearest address.

If you'd like to learn some of these powerful features in MapView, check out Apple's Development Forums and Guides–the possibilities are endless.

Chapter Summary

You've completed your sixth and final app as a part of this book. Congratulations! While developing this app, you used many different Swift features, including:

- Creating `UIAlertControllers`
- Adding text fields to Alert Controllers
- Creating action items for Alert Controllers
- Using action handlers
- Retrieving text field values from an alert controller
- Creating `CoreLocation` coordinates
- Creating `MapKit` spans
- Using `CLLocationCoordinates` and `MKCoordinateSpans` to create and set `MapKit` coordinate regions
- Adding frameworks to project dependencies
- Editing project `Info.Plist` files
- Creating a `CoreLocation` location manager
- Requesting user authorization for location usage
- Using the `locationManager(...didUpdateLocations...)` function for `CoreLocation`
- Adding `MKPointAnnotations` with specified coordinates
- Adding `UIGestureRecognizers`
- Specifying action selectors and using selector parameters
- Converting touch points to coordinate points through `MapKit`

After creating this multi-faceted application, you've gained another hand in becoming an advanced iOS developer. Through learning `MapKit`, `CoreLocation`, `UIAlerts` and `UIGestures`, you can now use these concepts to access users' locations and provide a more interactive interface in your applications. In addition to the geolocation features in this chapter, Swift also allows for many more features, including retrieving travel information, address information, etc. from the user. Other advanced structures in Swift, such as action handlers and functional selectors will also be key to creating some amazing apps, some of which you might even be able to publish.

See you in the last chapter!

Project Source Code

ViewController.swift

```
9    import UIKit
10
11   class ViewController: UIViewController, UITextFieldDelegate {
12       @IBOutlet weak var finalCurrency: UISegmentedControl!
13
14       @IBOutlet weak var initialCurrency: UISegmentedControl!
15
16       @IBOutlet weak var initialAmountTextField: UITextField!
17
18       @IBOutlet weak var finalAmountLabel: UILabel!
19
20       override func viewDidLoad() {
21           super.viewDidLoad()
22           // Do any additional setup after loading the view, typically from a nib.
23
24           initialAmountTextField.delegate = self
25       }
26
27       override func touchesBegan(_ touches: Set<UITouch>, with event: UIEvent?) {
28           self.view.endEditing(true)
29       }
30
31       @IBAction func buttonClicked(_ sender: Any) {
32           let initialAmount = Float(initialAmountTextField.text ?? "0") ?? 0
33           let initialCurrencyIndex = initialCurrency.selectedSegmentIndex
34           let finalCurrencyIndex = finalCurrency.selectedSegmentIndex
35
36           let finalAmount = convert(initialAmount: initialAmount, initialCurrencyIndex\
37   : initialCurrencyIndex, finalCurrencyIndex: finalCurrencyIndex)
38
39           finalAmountLabel.text = String(finalAmount)
40       }
41
42       func convert(initialAmount: Float, initialCurrencyIndex: Int, finalCurrencyIndex\
43   : Int) -> Float {
44           let factors = [1, 112, 0.86, 0.77] as [Float]
45
46           let initialFactor = factors[initialCurrencyIndex]
```

```
47          let finalFactor = factors[finalCurrencyIndex]
48
49          let finalAmount = initialAmount / initialFactor * finalFactor
50
51          return finalAmount
52      }
53
54      override func didReceiveMemoryWarning() {
55          super.didReceiveMemoryWarning()
56          // Dispose of any resources that can be recreated.
57      }
58
59
60  }
```

Chapter Fifteen: Finishing the Journey (Submitting Apps to the App Store)

Congratulations!

Congratulations on making it to the end of this book! This is just the beginning of your app development journey. Now that you've learned all of the basics of using Swift to create iOS applications, you should try to develop your first custom app, even if it's a bit basic. Each app you create will be better, and soon enough, your development practice will give you the skills to create an App Store-worthy app. Now that you've gotten a grasp of Swift's core concepts, you can use Apple's online libraries and other online resources to add onto your app development skillset.

In this chapter, I'll briefly cover the steps for submitting an app to the App Store. Each app will vary slightly in its process, since features such as In-App Purchases and TouchID will come with different additional steps.

Submiting Apps to the App Store

Joining the Apple Developer Program

1) First, navigate to `developer.apple.com` and log into your account (or a parent/guardian's account).

 To upload an app to the App Store, the holder of the Apple Account associated with the app must be over 18 years of age. If this does not apply to you, then you must use a parent's account. Joining the Apple Developer program also requires an enrollment fee of $99 USD per year.

2) After logging into your Apple ID, navigate to the `Account` tab, where a new page, such as the one in *Figure 15-1* will appear. On the bottom of this page, select "Join the Apple Developer Program."

Figure 15-1

3) Then, after pressing "Enroll" in the top-right-hand corner, follow the steps by inputting your personal infromation and selecting your payment methods. Enroll as an "Individual" unless the application you're creating is intended for corporate use.

Figure 15-2

Using the Apple Developer Dashboard

On the developer dashboard, you'll use a lot of features in the "Certificates, IDs & Profiles" tab and the "App Store Connect" tab:

Figure 15-3

Cerificates, Identifiers, and Profiles

Every app on the App Store requires Apple authorization and approval before any users can access or download it. Apple controls this process by assigning certificates and requiring that every device that runs an Apple-approved application has these certificates. If an app does not have a certificate that can be verified by the Apple device, the application will not function. Thus, iOS Developers need to thus create and sign certificates when they develop and release applications.

In this section of the Apple Developer Dashboard, you can create development and distribution "profiles," which are files that allow for code-signing whenever an app is idenified on a device.

- **Development profiles** are specifically tied to a certain set of devices, and are most often used when a developer needs to test an application.
- **Distribution profiles** are used to sign and verify an application before it is submitted for review on the App Store. They are used for non-specific devices.

App Store Connect

The App Store Connect is where all of the fun and exciting stuff is. In this tab, developers can register a new application, edit all of the information available on the App Store (such as screenshots, price, etc.), and then submit the application. This is also the tab where you can view analytics and trends for your applications.

Certificates, IDs, and Profiles

In this section, there are many steps that are necessary; some only need to be done once, whereas others must be done for every new app.

First, you'll need to create two certificates for your development and distribution profiles. Usually, Xcode can do this process, but it is important to understand the process to debug in the case that any problems occur.

Creating the Development Certificate

1) After pressing the tab for Certificates, IDs, and Profiles, you'll see the following page appear:

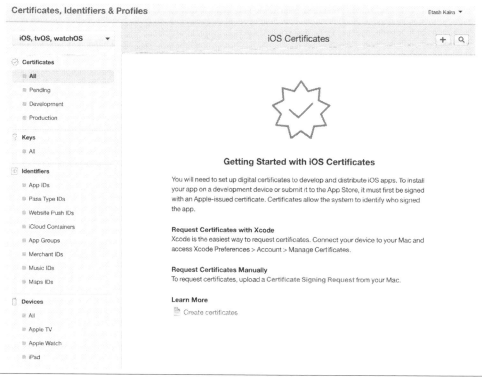

Figure 15-4

2) After selecting "iOS, tvOS, watchOS" in the top-left hand corner of the page, press the add (+) button in the top-right.

3) Under "Development," select the "iOS App Development" Certificate option.

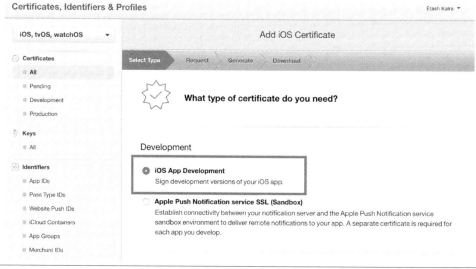

Figure 15-5

4) After pressing "Continue" on this page, follow the instructions given by Apple. You'll need to open the Keychain application on your computer, which can be found in the "Utilities" folder in "Applications," or by searching for it using the Mac Spotlight.

5) After creating a development certificate and saving it to your Mac's disk, navigate back to the Developer Dashboard, where you'll need to upload the certificate request file from your machine.

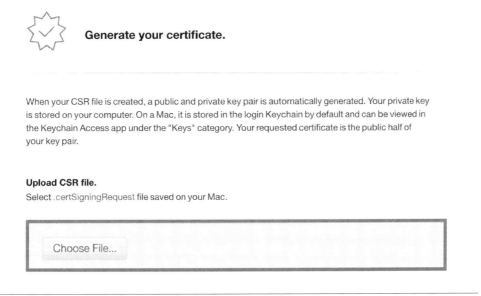

Figure 15-6

6) After uploading the request, Apple will generate a valid development certificate, which can be downloaded. Install this certificate on your machine by double clicking on it after downloading.

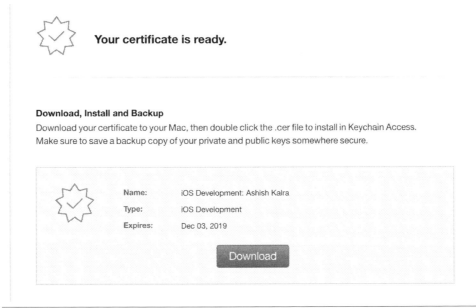

Figure 15-7

Creating the Distribution Certificate

After the development certificate, repeat the same steps from earlier, except by selecting an "App Store and Ad Hoc" certificate under the "Production" tab:

Production

⦿ **App Store and Ad Hoc**
   Sign your iOS app for submission to the App Store or for Ad Hoc distribution.

Figure 15-8

Download this certificate and add it to the system by double-clicking it.

 In case any certificates need to be re-installed by Xcode manually (even though they usually are installed automatically), you can download the file at the bottom of the certificates page, as shown in *Figure 15-9*:

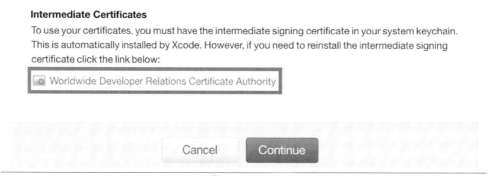

Intermediate Certificates
To use your certificates, you must have the intermediate signing certificate in your system keychain. This is automatically installed by Xcode. However, if you need to reinstall the intermediate signing certificate click the link below:

▣ Worldwide Developer Relations Certificate Authority

Cancel   Continue

Figure 15-9

Registering Devices

The next step, after creating certificates, is to register your devices as a developer. On the same screen, navigate to the "All Devices" tab on the left:

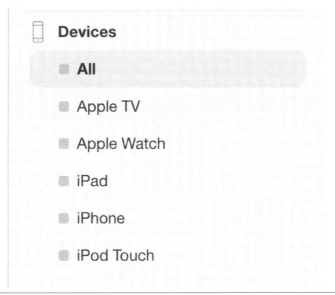

Figure 15-10

Using the add (+) button, add a new device with the device name and its unique UDID. The UDID can be found by plugging in your device into your Mac and launching iTunes:

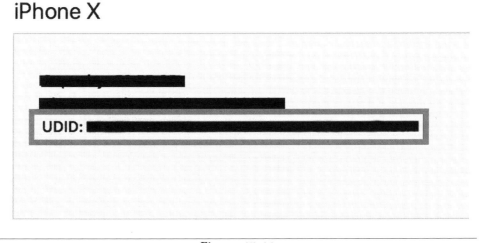

Figure 15-11

Creating an App ID

Every app you create, whether on the App Store or just locally on Xcode, requires a unique App ID. When we created an Xcode project, the name of project was used to create a unique App ID. If we wanted to, however, we could change the App ID in the Xcode IDE. On the developer site, navigate to the "Indentifiers > App IDs" tab using the left-bar.

App IDs are simply a combination of a prefix (specific to you as a developer) and a custom suffix, which defines the unique identifier for your application.

You usually won't be able to change App IDs without a lot of hassle and possibly creating a new app, so it is important to make sure that all of your App ID information is as accurate and consistent as possible.

On the top-right side of the screen, add a new Explicit App ID wih an identifier that matches the one on your Xcode project, and register that App ID.

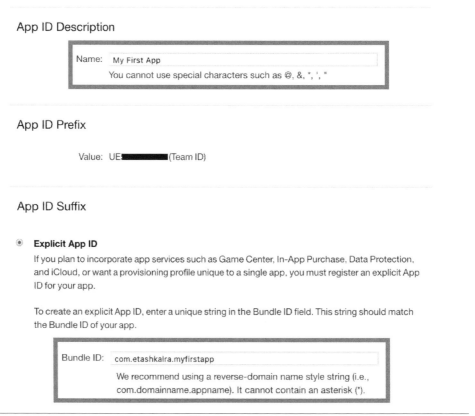

App ID Description

Name: My First App

You cannot use special characters such as @, &, *, ', "

App ID Prefix

Value: UE███████(Team ID)

App ID Suffix

○ **Explicit App ID**

If you plan to incorporate app services such as Game Center, In-App Purchase, Data Protection, and iCloud, or want a provisioning profile unique to a single app, you must register an explicit App ID for your app.

To create an explicit App ID, enter a unique string in the Bundle ID field. This string should match the Bundle ID of your app.

Bundle ID: com.etashkalra.myfirstapp

We recommend using a reverse-domain name style string (i.e., com.domainname.appname). It cannot contain an asterisk (*).

Figure 15-12

Provisioning Profiles

The final component of the "Certificates, Identifiers, and Profiles" sections is the Provisioning Profile, which combines the certificates we created, the device, and the App IDs. There are two types of provisioning profiles (development and distribution), just as there were two types of certificates.

Press the "All Provisioning Profiles" tab, and add a new one. Select "iOS App Development," and select the App ID, development certificate, and preferred device. Then, name the development profile and generate it. Go ahead and download the provisioning profile.

Do the same for an "App Store Distribution" profile. Double-clicking the downloaded files on your Mac will launch Xcode, confirming these development and distribution profiles.

Figure 15-13

After installing the provisioning profile, you should be able to run your applications on your devices and begin the App Store submission process!

App Store Connect

Getting Ready

On Xcode, confirm that you're signed into your Apple Developer Account. Select Xcode>Preferences in the application window bar, and select "Accounts." Signing in on Xcode allows for the provisioning profile to be shared from the developer console to your development project.

Additionally, check that your app is fully functional by pressing **Command** ⌘ and **B** keys to build it, and then **Command** ⌘ and **R** to run it. This can be done on the simulator or on your own registered device (preferrable).

Now, open the App Store Connect page, and navigate to the "Agreements, Tax, and Banking" page:

Figure 15-14

Here, set up all of the contact information for yourself (or a parent if under 18).

 Depending on the country, banking and tax information may be required (or not required) for free apps. All paid apps must have this information submitted.

Some Last Steps

Before submitting the app, there are a few key things you'll need ready:

- App Name
- App Description
- App Icon (various sizes for different devices)
- Screenshots for App Store Presentation

 The App Icon can be generated from a simple .png file using online app icon makers, which generate packages with different-sized icons for your apps. Your base icon must be at least 1024px by 1024px as of the current requirements.

After these have been created, navigate to the "My Apps" section of the App Store Connect page:

My Apps

Figure 15-15

Here, press + to create a new app, and input your basic application information, such as the platform, name, language, and bundle ID. For the SKU, input an identifier for the application that will be unique to your developer account (this will not be available for users to see).

New App

Platforms ?

☑ iOS   ☐ tvOS

Name ?

| My First App |

Primary Language ?

| English (U.S.)   ⌄ |

Bundle ID ?

| Choose   ⌄ |

Register a new bundle ID on the Developer Portal.

SKU ?

| FirstAppSKU102 |

User Access ?

○ Limited Access   ◉ Full Access

Figure 15-16

After creating the new app, input your app's information on the "App Information" page and then on the "Pricing and Availability" page:

Figure 15-17

Press save and click "Prepare for Submission," where you'll upload your app icons and screenshots, as well as any final pieces of information such as keywords for App Store searches.

 You can generate screenshots in the Xcode Simulator by pressing the **Command** ⌘ and **S** keys while your app is running. The simulator should be running in 100% scale mode.

Skip the "Build" section for now, but fill out the rest of the components on this page, such as the General App Information, Rating, and App Review Information. Save the page.

Final Submission

Before submitting the application in App Store Connect, the final step is adding the project build, which can be done from Xcode itself.

1) Go to Xcode, and in the device (scheme) selection, select "Generic iOS Device."

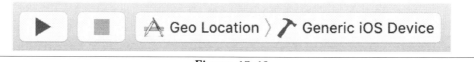

Figure 15-18

2) Then, Archive the project by using the application bar to select Product > Archive.

Figure 15-19

3) If the application is error-free, a new window will appear in which you can press the "Upload to

App Store" button. You can also validate the app again to confirm it's ready to go. The screen will also ask to confirm the certificates and provisioning profile you created earlier for this application.

4) After uploading, you'll receive a confirmation message. Now, navigate back to the developer page and refresh.

5) In the "Build" section, select the build you just uploaded via Xcode and press "Submit for Review." After answering a few questions, you'll be done! All that's left is your application approval.

Your Future

Great job on making your way through this book!

This is just the beginning of your app development journey.

Now that you have learned the basics, you should start creating your own apps right away. Even if it requires some advanced features not covered in this guide, you'll only learn those concepts by implementing them in your own applications. And, after some more practice, your second and third apps will undoubtedly be even better than your first.

Be sure to check out the Apple Development guides online to learn some of the newer features the Apple releases as a part of the Swift Development Kit. The guides also contain forums and protocols to handle any errors that you have while developing your apps.

Once again, contgratulations! Here's to your next amazing app.

Made in the USA
Lexington, KY
28 March 2019